LEADERSHIP, HAPPINESS & PROFIT

12 Steps to a High-Performance Business

TERRY "DOC" DOCKERY, Ph.D.

ISBN: 1500383139
ISBN-13: 978-1500383138

DEDICATION

To Cindy, Jill, Scott, and Lee –
the best decisions I ever made.

TABLE OF CONTENTS

Introduction

"Doc"trine #1: Harness Happiness

Part One: Everything Hinges on How You Think

- Harness the most powerful force in life
- Think your way to happiness and success
- Don't lose your balance
- Focus on the five things that create happiness
- Beware of the "retirement myth"

Part Two: What Makes People Tick?

- Use the secret to human motivation to your advantage
- Does your emotional bank account need a deposit?

Part Three: Harness Happiness for Profit

- Know the two best predictors of leadership success or failure
- Focus on primary pleasures
- Do you have a Chief Fun Officer?
- Beware of the Drama Triangle
- Increase happiness and productivity by increasing self-confidence
- Make sure your customers are happy

"Doc"trine #2: Be Someone Worth Following

- Good leaders are good parents
- The only real limitation on your business is you
- Honor the power of the truth
- Lead by example
- The trust-profit connection

- Blind spots? What blind spots?
- Beware of Profit Stealers ™

"Doc"trine #3: Focus Your Vision

- Don't waste your organizational energy
- You need an effective strategy *and* effective tactics
- "Embrace" the revised KISS Principle
- Focus on what's *really* important to your success
- Set achievable goals so you can "win"
- What kind of car is your business?
- A way to inspire creative visioning
- How to write a vision statement
- Can your business boat sail in a Blue Ocean for a while?
- How to write a mission statement
- How to stand out from your competitors
- Create the Strategic Priorities for your vision
- Decide on your Priority Actions for this year

"Doc"trine #4: Value Your Values

- Clear core values form a solid foundation for trusting relationships
- Don't succumb to greed—it will kill sustained business success
- How to create effective core values for your business
- How to use core values to drive business results
- Get rid of "terrorists"
- Decide if you want a religion-based business

"Doc"trine #5: Field a Pro Team

- If you want to win, field a pro team
- Feed your eagles
- How to identify "A" Players
- It's as easy as PIES ™!
- Recognize the Three Levels of Achievers ™

- Beware of "energy vampires"
- How to hire "A" Players
- How to be a great coach

"Doc"trine #6: Don't Turn Eagles into Turkeys

- Don't ask a quarterback to play lineman
- Help people succeed—fire them

"Doc"trine #7: Win with Win-Win

- Make sure your team reaches the "Performing" stage of development
- Do you have the right amount of team conflict?
- As a matter of fact, there IS an "I" in team: TEIM ™
- What's your roadmap for resolving conflicts constructively?
- "You catch more flies with honey…"
- How to get what you want in a conflict situation
- Think of sales as a special case of conflict resolution

"Doc"trine #8: Measure Success

- Measure what you want to get done
- Use this simple measure to get a bird's-eye view of your business
- Be a SKEPTIC about changes in your external environment
- SWOT those pesky ambiguities away
- Don't LIE ™ to yourself about the effectiveness of your processes
- Track the Core Success Measures
- Create a simple and manageable dashboard
- Create your Strategic Priorities Implementation Plan
- Align individual goals and business goals
- See all with 360 degree feedback

"Doc"trine #9: Clarify Roles and Accountability

- Don't try to hold a team accountable
- Design your organizational structure to fit your needs
- Create focused job descriptions
- Implement an effective performance management system

"Doc"trine #10: Delegate

- Don't be the "pinch point"
- Choose your decision-making style wisely
- Choose RAG(s) over riches
- How to delegate

"Doc"trine #11: Create Teamwork

- Create synergy in your team
- Do you have a leadership team or a leadership committee?
- Schedule recurring teamwork events
- Promote teamwork with your compensation plan
- For maximum motivation, use "open book" management

"Doc"trine #12: Institutionalize Innovation

- Build innovation into your business culture
- People support what they help create—empower them to be creative
- Take moderate business risks most of the time
- Build some "slack" into your business
- How to be creative through brainstorming
- Schedule recurring innovation events
- Plan for things to get harder before they get easier

Epilogue

References

Index

About the author

ACKNOWLEDGMENTS

Special thanks to Lynda McDaniel, Virginia McCollough, Emilee Annine Moeller, and Matt Boyd for all your help!

INTRODUCTION

A young man sat in disbelief, aching with disappointment. Sales and profits were both up, but he'd just been demoted from business manager back to salesman. What had he done wrong? Could he have done anything differently to avoid this pain and disappointment?

That young man was me. After that experience, I resolved to learn how to be a great leader who could guide a business on a path of sustained high performance. Nearly 30 years later, I can say that I kept that resolution—and more. I've helped scores of leaders go from stuck to unstuck, and I've watched them pursue and achieve their fondest business and personal goals.

Now it's time to pass on what I've learned. I wrote this book as a toolbox and field manual for leaders who want to build sustainable high-performance businesses. If that's your goal, this book will help you achieve it. If you follow these principles, you will be successful, and even more importantly, happy beyond your wildest imaginings. I promise this has been true for so many of my clients, so stay with me here. This book includes top concepts that have the highest impact on a leader's success and happiness. That's right—happiness. After all, what good is all the business success in the world if you're not happy?

Also, if you're a business owner (or hopefully at least thinking like one), please note that the principles explained throughout this book apply regardless of your business exit strategy. Having the right people, plan, and processes in place will maximize the value of your business, making it easier and more profitable to sell if and when that time comes.

Valuing wisdom

Over my career, I've seen dozens of leadership and management and fads come and go. So many leaders seem to spend their time looking for the latest and greatest "silver bullet" that will create amazing success with a single shot. I have good news and bad news: it's not as simple as a silver bullet, but it's much simpler than many (mostly consultants) would have you believe.

The premise

I start with the premise that there's a huge difference between knowledge and wisdom. I'm a big fan of wisdom—and it doesn't have an expiration date. That's why you'll see some of the greatest thinkers of our time referenced in this book. Of course, I share my own experience and insights, too. My goal is to share the best wisdom I know, and I'm not particularly concerned about who gets the credit. Sometimes it's difficult to identify what is intellectual property and what falls into public domain, but I've attempted to document the sources of the concepts as best I can.

I'm also a big fan of common sense. Getting my Ph.D. in Industrial/Organizational Psychology almost did me in. While I saw clearly the value of pure research, I discovered that hyper-focused detailed analysis was not what I was passionate about. By the time I walked away with that degree in my hand, I wondered if I needed to conduct a six-month, double-blind study to decide if I needed to use the restroom.

Business leaders live in a world that moves at warp speed, and they often need to make decisions quickly. They need to combine detailed data analysis with feelings and intuition to make the best decisions, so I'll ask my academic colleagues to consider my life's work in this book as a longitudinal case study that has produced techniques and results worthy of their attention. The best decisions are made by combining your thoughts with your feelings and intuition, aren't they? Why shortchange yourself by using only a portion of your assets?

My promise

I'd like to help you be happier, make more money, and do more good. It's what I've done for clients for over 20 years, and I'd like to do the same for you, my readers. As I mentioned earlier, I particularly want to help you be happier and more successful at work (and it naturally follows that you'll be happier and more successful in the rest of your life, too).

The 12 leadership "Doc"trines can also boost your profits through better practices and more innovation. And doing good? You'll read that doing good (e.g., making a positive difference in the lives of others by providing a valuable product or service in the marketplace) is one of the five primary sources of happiness, and that happy people (including you) are essential to sustained financial performance.

As you read through the "Doc"trines, you'll see stories and references to my work in the field. I believe that sharing my experience and opinions about what works well to achieve results is the best way to make this book worth your time. Anyone can cite the research (or you can look it up yourself), but I want you to have the benefit of my victories and defeats over decades of study, research, and consulting.

After all, why should you have to reinvent the wheel? I've already made many of the mistakes that you may be about to make, so take advantage of this opportunity to capitalize on what I've learned through working with a host of organizations. I've also placed some graphics in the book, including some hand-drawn originals by my friend Matt Boyd that I hope will make the concepts more enjoyable and more memorable.

In the movie Cool Hand Luke, our hero Luke, played by Paul Newman, is a rebellious prisoner who has run away several times from the chain gang and endures back-breaking punishment for this when he's caught.

As the scene opens, Luke is at the bottom of a five-by-five-foot hole he's just dug with a shovel, filled in, and now is digging again. It's nighttime, and Luke has been at this for untold hours. He's drenched in sweat and well past exhaustion. He pleads with the guard watching him to stop the punishment and pain, and the guard says, "Do you have your mind right now, Luke?"

With tearful eyes and quivering voice, Luke says, "Yeah, boss, I've got my mind right."

I've seen too many leaders who are also "down in a hole" in terms of their limited thinking and knowledge about how to get extraordinary business results. It doesn't have to be that way. Today, we have a wealth of information about leadership that can make you as happy and as successful as you've ever dreamed. Let's "get our minds right" and stop the needless pain—the rest will be easy. We just might feel as good as Luke did when he climbed out of that hole and began planning to escape his limiting prison altogether.

So what do you say we identify what works well and use it to be happy, make money, and do some good out there in the business world? If you like, you can start by taking five minutes to complete the 12-item Leading Indicator Evaluation TM on the next page. It will tell you quickly where the strengths and opportunities for performance improvement are in your business.

LEADING INDICATOR EVALUATION™

Please rate your leadership team from 1 to 5 on how it is currently performing.

1 = Failing = F
2 = Below Average = D
3 = Average = C
4 = Above Average = B
5 = Excellent = A

LEADING INDICATOR	"A" STANDARD	Rating
Harness happiness	Members are happy & motivated	
Be someone worth following	Our leaders are great examples	
Field a pro team	Members are top 10% performers in their roles, or can be soon	
Don't turn eagles into turkeys	Members' roles fit their talents well	
Win with win-win	Conflicts are resolved effectively	
Focus your vision	Goals are clear, focused, & prioritized	
Value your values	Core values are followed consistently	
Measure success	We are measuring the right things	
Delegate	Authority is delegated effectively	
Clarify roles & accountability	Roles & accountabilities are clear, follow through is consistent	
Create teamwork	High level of teamwork & synergy	
Institutionalize innovation	High level of continuous innovation	
TOTAL		
OVERALL AVERAGE SCORE (Total divided by 12)		
OVERALL PERFORMANCE "GRADE" 1 = F, 2 = D, 3 = C, 4 = B 4.5 = A		

"DOC"TRINE #1: HARNESS HAPPINESS

The drive for happiness is the most powerful force in life—harness it for business success.

The Payoff

You're happy, your employees are happy, and your customers are happily buying your products and services (and you thought having a Chief Fun Officer was a silly idea…).

"Doc"trine #1 in Action: Union-Management Kumbaya

A manufacturing plant had been losing money for 20 years, and in that time, the plant had been owned by four different corporations. Everyone agreed that the main problem was an adversarial relationship between the management and union leadership teams. Nobody was really happy with the situation and mutual contempt and sneers were the order of the day. The list of consulting colleagues and members of both leadership teams who told me that we would never succeed in making a positive difference would have stretched out the door and around the block.

A union-management contract "negotiating" session looked more like a bar room brawl, and we were constantly concerned that someone from the union team was going to reach across the table and smack someone from the management team. I lay awake at night in my hotel room wondering why I hadn't chosen to be something safer, perhaps a mercenary in a war zone. I even created a new conflict resolution technique to get people laughing so they would be less tempted to strangle each other!

We conducted a series of individual interviews with the members of the union and management leadership teams to hear their concerns and their recommendations to improve the situation. Then we conducted four days of team meetings. First, we spent a full day each with the union and then the management leadership teams to help them clarify their respective goals, values, and recommendations for improvement at the plant. Then we brought the two leadership teams together for the last two days.

On the first morning, I would have felt safer as a lion tamer entering a cage full of hungry predators. This was compounded by a spindly flip chart easel that tended to fall over every time I tried to write on the flip chart and a cavernous meeting room approximately the size of Montana. It was almost impossible to read the written flip chart pages without binoculars once they were hung on the distant walls.

But we persevered. We compared our two lists of goals, values, and recommendations, and lo and behold, they were virtually identical! This led to a group epiphany and "eureka!" moment that created goose bumps all around! It turned out that we all wanted the same thing—it just had gotten lost in all the past miscommunication, misunderstanding, and mistrust.

It was the business equivalent of singing Kumbaya arm-in-arm. The excitement in the room was palpable as everyone began to see the possibilities for dramatically improving everyone's success and happiness. We spent the rest of our time together creating a happier and more profitable future for the plant.

PART ONE: EVERYTHING HINGES ON HOW YOU THINK!

Harness the most powerful force in life

First, let's start with the end in mind. Isn't the whole point of being a good leader and making a good profit to be happy? Aristotle and I would argue that the whole point of being alive is to be happy, so that's step one. Think of happiness as a 200-foot tsunami bearing down on you. It makes no sense to fight something so powerful—it will just crush you. Instead, hop on your surfboard and ride that wave to business and personal success!

Second, the foundation of a profitable business is happy people: you, your partners, your employees, and your customers. As an added bonus, it turns out that leveraging happiness as a competitive business advantage is so infrequently done well that it becomes a very powerful differentiator in your marketplace to help you generate impressive profits (e.g., think Southwest Airlines or Zappos).

Third, I've never seen a business with an unhappy leader or with unhappy employees that has happy customers, much less sustained high performance. Of course happiness can't be a substitute for long-term productivity and profit (lagging indicator), but it is most definitely a precursor to achieving them (leading indicator), as well as the ultimate lagging indicator.

MAKE HAPPINESS THE DRIVING FORCE OF YOUR BUSINESS

A happy you

⬇

Happy followers

⬇

Happy customers

⬇

Happy profits

Decide you're going to lead a happy life. Don't settle for less, and don't listen to those who tell you otherwise (e.g., "life is suffering," "life isn't fair," "you're expecting too much"). Life can be all those things at times, but your basic choices are to be a:

1. Creator of Happiness, or
2. Critic of Creators

Guess which folks are happier and more successful? Be realistic in your expectations, but focus more on the positive than the negative.

Rate your happiness every day. Use any scale you want (e.g., 1 = below average, 2 = average, 3 = above average; or 0-10 with 5 being average), but assign a number to your level of happiness to keep your focus on what's working and what's not working in your life as a person and as a leader. If you see a downward trend over time, then you know it's time for some changes. If your ratings stay high, then keep doing what you're doing!

High-performance habit: Consciously choose how you think.

Think your way to happiness and success

How we think is how we feel is how we act is the results we get.

YOUR DAILY SELF-FULFILLING PROPHECY

How you think

How you feel

How you act

The results you get

If you start off thinking unhappy and negative thoughts, the rest is pretty predictable. By in large, how you think determines how you feel. Behavioral therapists have used this fact to help people for decades. Of course, if you step in front of a moving bus or you're very hungry, then you're thinking isn't the primary cause of your feelings. But those are the exception; most of the time we create our feelings by what we think. For example, if you spend a lot of time thinking about the past and how much you miss something, you will feel sad. If instead you think about the future and how much you are looking forward to something, then you will feel happy.

Our union and management teams from the beginning of the chapter spent a lot of time brooding over perceived past "injustices" and kept themselves feeling hurt, angry, and combative. Once we focused on common values and goals and how to create a happier future, they began to feel excited and optimistic about the idea of working together as a team.

There's a lot in life that we can't control, but we can control the way we think. And that's great because it's the most powerful tool we have to create success and happiness. Many people never fully realize this and don't take full advantage of their ability to take greater control over their lives and their happiness.

Not only is personal karma at play in the world, but leadership karma and business karma also affect your life. If you create positive energy and share it with the world, it truly will come back to you. This isn't a mystical wish; it's a practical reality. There isn't a one-to-one correlation between what you put out and what you get back, but at the big picture level, it always works!

Let's revisit the case of the Union-Management Brawl at the beginning of the chapter. Both the union and management leaders assumed that the other side was out to do them harm. Based on these beliefs they acted in an adversarial fashion toward each other, assuming there would be one winner and one loser. Essentially these leaders were broadcasting a great deal of negativity and distrust.

Sure enough, as in any good self-fulfilling prophecy, their expectations were borne out because the other side responded with their own negativity and distrust. Once we established the true values and goals of both groups and discovered that they were very similar, the leaders generated a new set of assumptions and broadcasted more positive energy and trust. This built the foundation for all our subsequent success as that positive energy was returned and reciprocated many times over.

High-performance habit: Believe that what you put out into the world will come back to you, both positive and negative.

Abraham Lincoln was right when he said, "A man is about as happy as he makes his mind up to be." (Please forgive Abe for his sexist language; those were the times.) I've done a lifetime of personal research, and I can testify that, to a huge degree, what you focus on determines how happy you are with your life.

I know you may be weary of hearing about the power of positive thinking, but seriously, it just plain works. Life can provide plenty of unhappiness any time you need some. In fact, if you really want to feel unhappy, just turn on the evening news and those folks will bring you all the misery in the world in 30 minutes in a format that you can't control. By contrast, if you don't want to feel unhappy, I recommend that you get your news in another format in which you are not forced to watch all that misery with no control over how it is presented.

Let's extend this analogy: Imagine your life as a movie. If you watch sad movies all day (i.e., what you actually watch, what you actually think), then you will feel unhappy. If you watch happy movies all day, then you will feel happy. It's what you focus on, or the movie you show yourself that makes the difference. What's playing at your personal movie theater?

I'm not advocating a rose-colored Pollyanna perspective that is based on denying unhappiness in the world. Sure, there will always be unhappiness in the world, but if you can't fix it, then why focus on it?

I once heard a client who was millionaire complaining that he was a total failure because he wasn't a billionaire. Who could make this stuff up? Talk about a "glass half empty" kind of guy…

High-performance habit: Focus on the positive.

We're all concerned about world peace (well, some of us are), but it's awfully hard to control. One of my favorite quotes is, "For true peace of mind, resign as Master of the Universe." The author is unknown, but she sure had her thinking cap on that day.

For a graphic presentation of this idea, see Stephen Covey's Circle of Concern/Circle of Influence model (Covey, 1992) in the figure below.

FOCUS ON WHAT YOU CAN CONTROL

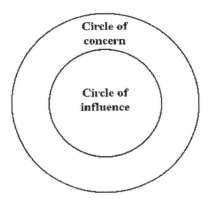

We can use our circle of influence to impact our circle of concern, but gnashing our teeth over the absence of world peace will only cause us unproductive heartache and misery, which ironically lessens our ability to influence world peace. Instead, practice the Serenity Prayer from Alcoholics Anonymous:

"Grant me the serenity to accept the things I cannot change, the courage to change the things I can, and the wisdom to know the difference."

High-performance habit: Focus on what you can control.

Don't lose your balance

The Greeks had it right when they said, "All things in moderation." Many of the best decisions in running a high-performance business are based on choosing/justifying the right balance between two extremes.

And research has shown that people who are successful over the long term tend to take a moderate level of risk. They don't avoid risk, but they don't "swing for the fence" on a regular basis either. Assertiveness needs moderation, too. Everyone knows that being too passive can limit your happiness and success. However, being overly assertive can make you mean and domineering (like the union and management leaders in our case study), which will limit your happiness and success. Consider the Principle of PB&J below and you won't find yourself in a "jam" nearly as often:

THE PRINCIPLE OF BALANCE & JUSTIFICATION (PB&J) ™

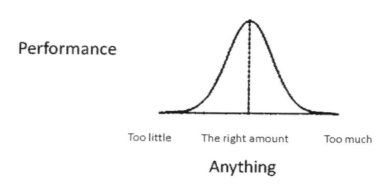

High-performance habit: Keep a balanced perspective—beware of extremism.

Focus on the five things that create happiness

Research from the field of Positive Psychology (and common sense) tells us that there are five major sources of happiness.

1. Good health
2. Enough money to pay your bills and have some left over for fun

3. Work that is interesting, challenging, and enjoyable
4. Caring relationships with others
5. Making a difference in the lives of others

High-performance habit: Focus on the five sources of happiness in your life.

For your career happiness, choose a career you feel passionate about. That's what you want to focus your efforts on, because this "fit" between you and your career is enormously important. That's how you can be happiest and most successful in the world. Think about it. If you aren't guided by your passions, or what makes you feel good (versus what makes you feel bad), what are you going to base your life decisions on? There are three main reasons that choosing a career you're passionate about is a good idea:

1. There are thousands of ways to make a buck. If you choose a business that you are passionate about, it allows you to focus in an otherwise overwhelming sea of choices.
2. When you run into hard times, which we all do from time to time, your passion will sustain you and give you the energy you need to persevere and succeed. If you're just going through the motions at something you don't care deeply about, quitting and failing become a more tolerable—and likely—option.
3. If despite your best efforts the business were to fail, you will have spent your time learning valuable lessons while doing something that you love. Then you can use these valuable lessons and your banked happiness to succeed at your next venture.

Decide you're going to have a happy and profitable career. Once again, don't settle for less; focus on the positive, and don't listen to those who tell you otherwise (e.g., "the majority of startups are out of business within two years," "you can't get anything done in a corporate setting because of all the bureaucracy" [yada, yada, yada…]).

You have four basic career choices:

1. Work for someone else
    a. Pros: Predictable income, a built-in team environment, the opportunity to learn from seasoned leaders.
    b. Cons: You always have a boss whose weaknesses constrain your opportunities.
2. Solopreneur
    a. Pros: You are the boss, financial and personal growth opportunities are unlimited, complete control over your schedule and priorities.
    b. Cons: Can be lonely (especially if you're an extrovert), financial risk.
3. Entrepreneur Owner-Operator
    a. Pros: You are the boss, you hand pick your team, your financial and personal growth opportunities are unlimited, complete control over your schedule and priorities.
    b. Cons: Most of your time is spent working in the business, leaving little time for other career pursuits, financial risk.
4. Entrepreneur Owner.
    a. Pros: You can leverage your business savvy to create a variety of businesses that you own without most of your time spent in any one business, financial and personal growth opportunities are unlimited, complete control over your schedule and priorities.
    b. Cons: Financial risk

Many leaders, at one time or another, find themselves in all four of these roles. The CEO of a professional services company I worked with started out as a leader in a well-respected company in his industry. He was downsized out, needed work, and started his own business. As he became more successful and more confident in his leadership and business skills, he acquired other companies and hired leaders to run them.

High-performance habit: Choose a career lifestyle that is the best "fit" for you—you'll never be truly happy if you don't.

Beware of the "retirement myth"

Lastly, beware what I call the "retirement myth." Especially here in the United States, we tend to work too hard during our careers and promise ourselves that we'll have time to do all those things we'd really like to do (e.g., travel, spend more time with friends and family) when we retire. All too often this strategy turns out to be tragically flawed.

We don't enjoy our career as much as we might because we're chronically overworked, and then by the time we retire we've damaged our health to the point that we can't enjoy our retirement as we'd planned. In addition, we discover that having complete freedom to do whatever we want (especially "doing nothing") isn't the key to happiness that we thought it would be. We realize that the key to happiness and success is about enjoying good health, living in balance, being involved with others, and making a real difference in the world. The plan to work too hard in the beginning and rest up at the end turns out to be a huge mistake. You'd be amazed how many times retired leaders have told me, "You know, you can only play so much golf before it gets boring."

High-performance habit: Beware the "retirement myth"—insist on being happy your whole life.

PART TWO: WHAT MAKES PEOPLE TICK?

Use the secret to human motivation to your advantage

Sigmund Freud truly was a genius. He created the best model of explaining and predicting human behavior ever. Eric Berne was not shabby, either. He created Transactional Analysis, which added more understandable names and everyday examples to Freud's model to make it more useful for business people like you and me. See the figure below.

THE SECRET TO HUMAN MOTIVATION

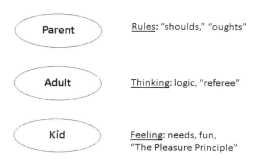

Parent	<u>Rules</u>: "shoulds," "oughts"
Adult	<u>Thinking</u>: logic, "referee"
Kid	<u>Feeling</u>: needs, fun, "The Pleasure Principle"

<u>The Secret</u>: The Kid never grows up

There are three separate parts to our personalities. Going from the bottom up on the figure, first is the "Kid," which is the basic healthy animal in us. The Kid is composed of basic needs (e.g., food, water, shelter, intimacy with others) and lives by "The Pleasure Principle." That is, kids just want to feel good, have fun, and enjoy life. What could be healthier and simpler?

Imagine a six-month old baby. He is feeling happy, and then he gets hungry. He cries, he gets fed, and he is happy again. Life is good. Now let's make him six years old. He is happy, and then he gets hungry at 5 p.m. He is about to run headlong into the second part of our personalities, the "Parent."

Let's say that only his mother is home, and she is preparing dinner in the next room. He asks her, "Mom, I'm hungry. May I have something to eat?" She says, "I'm sorry, honey, but I'm going to have to say 'no.' One of the rules we live by is that we eat dinner as a family at 6 p.m., so you'll just have to wait."

Now the Kid is frustrated. He didn't want to feed the whole family; he just wanted a bite to eat to tide him over until dinner so he doesn't get a headache. What we have now is a conflict between the needs of the Kid and the rules of the Parent. We all know that some cultural rules or agreements for behavior are helpful (e.g., laws against running stop lights or murdering other people), but the Kid in our story is still left to decide how to solve his hunger problem in his family, which is the first culture he is exposed to. Thus he calls on the third part of our personalities, the "Adult."

Our Adult is capable of rational and analytical thought, and our Adult often becomes the referee between the needs of the Kid and the rules of our Parent (whether our real parent or the Parent in our head that becomes part of us). In our example, our Kid's Adult starts to do what he does best—think. "Let's see. I can think of a couple of ideas. Mom is on that healthy eating kick. Maybe I can talk her into giving me a granola bar because it is 'healthy' food. Or maybe I can sneak a cookie out of the cookie jar without Mom seeing me. Either way, nobody gets hurt, and I don't have to be hungry and unhappy for the next hour."

How is this knowledge useful in running your business, you ask? The basic principle and secret to human motivation is this—our Kids never grow up. We have the same needs (plus some other social ones that come with adolescence) that we did when we were six years old. Hopefully we just get wiser about how to meet these needs over time.

If you're making decisions using only the "rational adult" model that you were taught in school, then you're missing much of the big picture. If the majority of the world's people operated on the rational adult model, there would be no war, no poverty, and no murder, and all business strategic plans would be created and implemented flawlessly. For example, logically it may sound good to cut all your employees' pay by 20% so you can lower your overhead expenses, but the subsequent emotional responses of those employees likely wouldn't get you the profitability results you were thinking of.

As another example, if you've ever known an employee who is an alcoholic, you must know that she didn't sit down one day and decide it was in her best interests to be an alcoholic. Therefore, this was not a rational (Adult) decision. Instead, this is someone trying to cope with some emotional need (Kid) that is not being met a healthier way.

Think about some leadership decisions in which this model can help you predict someone's behavior or respond to behavioral issues. For example, what if one of your employees is chronically late? Surely the Adult part of that person knows that this behavior is irritating to the people who have to wait on him; he also knows that this may result in perceptions of unreliability and untrustworthiness, as well as a lack of support for things that are important to him over time.

It's easy to threaten consequences for this behavior, but it might be to your advantage to ask yourself, "What emotional need is behind this seemingly self-destructive behavior, and what clever action might I take to address that need?" Of course, it would be ideal if he would just tell you, but he might not know consciously.

Perhaps he dislikes attending meetings in your business because they are boring and unproductive (what, you say, not my meetings!), so he's either consciously or unconsciously avoiding them because they aren't any fun or a good use of his time. In this instance, structuring more effective meetings would be an easy fix to the chronic tardiness problem. Or maybe he dislikes his job altogether and that would require a bigger fix of some kind. Remember, Kids just want to have fun. Let them!

High-performance habit: Remember that "the kid" in us never grows up—if behavior isn't rational, then it must be emotional.

Does your emotional bank account need a deposit?

There is an "emotional economy" in your life. For example, you make a deposit by scheduling time with your family and friends, by taking regular vacations, or by setting achievable goals you can accomplish and feel good about. Okay, now your emotional account is in good shape. Then you work extra- long hours for several weeks because of a big project. Now your emotional account is depleted because you're feeling tired and burnt out.

The moral of the story is to keep investing in your emotional economy and in that of your employees. I've noticed that leaders who are men often think that feelings don't matter, and that we can operate regularly with a bankrupt personal emotional economy. Don't believe this for a second; there's no way to beat the system. Your creditors (emotions) will harass you until you pay up. You can do it the easy way, or you can do it the hard way (e.g., health problems, divorce, emotional problems), but the bill will come due regardless. Note that the union and management leaders in our case study for this chapter were all about business, but the emotional bank accounts on both sides were badly in need of a "deposit" of happiness and job satisfaction.

PART 3: HARNESS HAPPINESS FOR PROFIT

Know the two best predictors of leadership success or failure

For more than 20 years, The Ohio State Studies (1945-1970s) examined the factors leading to leadership success. The results showed that the two factors that best predicted leadership success or failure are:

1. **Consideration:** caring whether your teammates are happy.
2. **Initiating Structure:** planning and decreasing ambiguity in goals, roles, and values.

Consideration was the best single predictor of leadership success by a wide margin. So, contrary to what you might believe, it's not financial acumen, market analysis, or being tough minded that gets the best business results. All these things can be important at times, but leadership success and business success are both driven primarily by the ability to form good relationships with others (e.g., teammates and customers).

The way you form good relationships with others is to show them that you care about them (i.e., are considerate). This is true whether these relationships are face-to-face or virtual, and it's especially true if you want people to follow you willingly. Take a moment to think about all the charismatic leaders you are aware of, and you'll see that this is a common trait they share.

This approach works even when the leaders are misguided, as in the cases of Adolph Hitler or Jim Jones. Their followers truly believed that these men cared about their happiness and trusted that they would look out for their best interests. If it works this well for deranged leaders, imagine how well it can work for you!

High-performance habit: Make sure your followers know you care about them—in return they will care about you and your business.

Focus on Primary Pleasures ™

I'm sure you've heard the old saying, "The most important things in life are free." I know from experience with scores of clients that it's true, even when your goal is to build a business with sustained financial high performance. If your plan for happiness and success isn't built on a solid foundation of primary pleasures, then you'll find that making a lot of money will leave you feeling disappointed and unfulfilled.

The basic primary pleasures are:

1. Good health
2. A good relationship with yourself
3. Good relationships with others

The secondary pleasures are:

1. Money
2. Power
3. Status

Think about it. If you don't have your basic health and happiness, then all the money, power, and status in the world are meaningless. There is no amount of secondary pleasures that will replace a lack of primary pleasures in your life. Ask those who have lost their health, their self-esteem, or their family and friends.

In a similar vein, Abraham Maslow (1929) did some fascinating work on the hierarchy of human needs (see figure below).

MASLOW'S NEED HIERARCHY

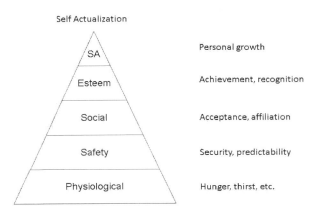

Without delving deeply into Maslow's theory, the basic idea is that it's hard to get yourself or anybody else to pay attention to a goal, such as achievement at work, if they don't already feel reasonably physically safe and cared about.

I've lost count of how many times I've heard leaders say things like, "He's lazy, and he doesn't care about the company," when in fact the person has no good reason to care about the company. He's being treated like a minion, or worse, an idiot, and his needs and happiness are not being attended to, and he doesn't have any financial incentives to increase his performance. And yet he's supposed to "act like an owner" and care about the performance of the whole company. Good luck getting results with that leadership approach—you'll need it!

Douglas McGregor (1960) said there are two basic leadership philosophies of human behavior at work: Theory X, those leaders who believe people are basically "lazy," and Theory Y, those leaders who are motivated only by "the carrot and the stick" or short-term rewards (e.g., a bonus) and punishments (e.g., the threat of firing). Those leaders who believe Theory Y think that people are naturally industrious and are motivated by higher-order desires such as being part of a winning team or developing their personal skills.

In my experience, Theory Y leaders get much better results. I've found that most people are capable of much more than liking carrots and fearing sticks. In our case study for this chapter, both the union and management leaders assumed the worst motivations about each other, and no one felt safe and secure enough to focus fully on organizational high performance and profitability. High-performance habit: Make sure employees' basic needs are met (like safety) so they can focus on higher-order needs (like profit).

Remember the five basic sources of happiness? Use this knowledge to your advantage by building them into your business. For example, offer your employees:

1. **Good health:** Provide a fitness facility or programs and healthy snacks.
2. **Enough money to pay bills and have some left over for fun:** Pay fair market value compensation, pay for performance, practice "open book management."
3. **Work that is interesting, challenging, and enjoyable:** Delegate authority, grant autonomy, cross train.
4. **Caring relationships with others:** Reward teamwork, promote teambuilding activities, create a mentoring program.
5. **Making a difference in the lives of others:** Include your contribution to society as part of your business mission statement, create a volunteer civic-engagement program to give back to your community.

If you're not focusing on the things that make you and others happy, what are you focusing on?

Do you have a Chief Fun Officer?

Appoint a Chief Fun Officer for your business. If you have a Vice President of Human Resources, why not appoint them as the Chief Fun Officer for your business? Or appoint someone else who monitors the morale and motivation of your employees and helps to keep their spirits high. Make sure that the basics are covered (e.g., recognition, autonomy, growth opportunities, fair pay, competitive benefits) before expending resources on teambuilding activities (e.g., pizza parties, ballgames). Both are important—but in that order.

I once worked with a startup business that was a spinoff from an existing business. Sitting with the leadership team in our strategic planning session, the group was certain that they wanted to create a business culture that was very different from that of the parent company. They had come from a culture that rewarded people for being overly cautious and fearful of change and failure, and they wanted to create a culture that was more fun, engaging, and innovative. When we broached the idea of appointing a Chief Fun Officer to insure that people were engaged and happy in their work, I was nearly trampled in a stampede of those who wanted to occupy the role!

As with many variables, stress and work performance are related in a bell shaped curve (see figure below).

OPTIMUM STRESS LEVEL FOR MAXIMUM PERFORMANCE

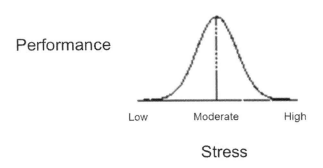

Performance

Low   Moderate   High

Stress

With too little stress, most of us are bored because we like a challenge. At moderate stress levels individuals are engaged and motivated to achieve. At very high stress levels, especially over a long period, people feel overwhelmed and discouraged and performance goes down again.

We've explored how your happiness and success are in direct relation to your employees' happiness. But you're busy, so how can you tell if they're happy or not? Ask them. For example, conduct employee-engagement surveys every 6 to12 months. Also ask employees regularly what's making them happy and motivated, and what's making them unhappy and unmotivated.

High-performance habit: Measure your employees' happiness regularly.

Beware of the Drama Triangle

When people aren't happy overall, we start to see some unusual but predictable behavior, which is well described by the Drama Triangle (Karpman, 1968).

THE DRAMA TRIANGLE

Victim

Rescuer   Persecutor

People who choose to stay in an unhappy business environment become dissatisfied and start to feel like Victims. (e.g., "Life is difficult and unfair, and I have little or no control over my own happiness.") Their thinking is accurate in that they often don't have the authority in the business to change the things that are making them unhappy (e.g., a perfectionistic, demanding supervisor who can't be pleased). Staying in this environment can lead them to a sense of "learned helplessness," (Seligman, 1975) in which they become convinced that they cannot change their lives to become happier.

As the boss in this situation, you'll likely be seen (often quite rightly) as the Persecutor who is creating this unhappiness. You'll also begin to notice a lot of secretive, third-party meetings that tend to be conducted in whispered tones. That's when Rescuers inevitably will emerge to try to console and counsel the Victim and commiserate about what an awful Persecutor boss you are.

But it gets even more dramatic when people inevitably begin to change roles on the triangle. For example, Rescuers will encourage Victims to be more assertive with their supervisors (maybe you) to address their concerns. Then the Victims get angry (e.g., "What are you trying to do, get me fired? You don't care about me, and we can't be friends anymore!") and move to the Persecutor role. That leads to their Rescuers becoming the Victims in the situation. This can lead to a nasty cycle that ultimately leads to you, the leader, becoming the real victim because of all the lost productivity and costly turnover of good employees that you will experience.

In our union and management case study, almost everyone was unhappy. The members of management team felt like "Victims" because they believed the union's "Persecutors" were purposefully sabotaging their efforts to run a happy and profitable business. So the members of the management team moved into the role of "Persecutors" and started treating the union people harshly and without respect. The union people then felt like "Victims," and called on the International Union to help them ("Rescuers"). The International Union then became the "Persecutors" of the management team and they again moved to the "Victims" position. Now we've come full circle (and wasted a great deal of time, money, and potential happiness).

Some takeaways here include:

1. Hire people who are basically happy and productive.
2. Create a business environment where people can be happy and productive.
3. If you don't, you'll lose your best employees to costly turnover—they won't stay in an unhappy environment.

Increase happiness and productivity by increasing self-confidence

There are two primary ways to increase your self-confidence and your employees' self-confidence so you can accomplish more:

1. **Master new skills.** When people master new skills, they feel more confident that they can handle whatever business (and life) throws at them. Support professional development programs for every individual on your team.
2. **Lower your standards.** "Stretch goals" can be overdone. Set achievable goals so you and your team can feel as though you're winning. The added confidence will inspire people to tackle even more challenging goals.

This is exactly what happened in our case study. The union and management teams began to set reasonable goals together and build new skills, and they then had the confidence to take on ever more challenging goals of productivity and profitability.

High-performance habit: Increase self-confidence by mastering new skills or lowering your standards.

Make sure your customers are happy

Don't forget the happiness level of your customers! You can ask them regularly in your interactions, and/or you can conduct a customer satisfaction/loyalty survey every six months. Never forget they are the lifeblood of your business. The graveyard of failed businesses is littered with those companies whose leaders lost sight of this simple principle. Look at Eastman Kodak. Their customers wanted digital photography, but Kodak kept trying to sell them print photography. Wrong move…

High-Performance Habits Checklist

- ☐ Consciously choose how you think.
- ☐ Believe that the energy you put out into the world will come back to you, both positive and negative.
- ☐ Focus on the positive, what you can control, and the five sources of happiness
- ☐ Keep a balanced perspective—beware extremism.
- ☐ Choose a career lifestyle that is the best "fit" for your passions and talents.
- ☐ Beware the "retirement myth"—insist on being happy your whole life.
- ☐ Remember that "the kid" in us never grows up—if behavior isn't rational, then it must be emotional.
- ☐ Make sure your followers know you care about them--in return they'll care about you and your business.
- ☐ Make sure basic needs are met (like safety) so employees can focus on higher-order needs (like profit).
- ☐ Measure your employees' and your customers' happiness regularly.
- ☐ To maximize productivity, hire happy people and give them a happy work environment.
- ☐ If you see "Drama Triangle" behaviors among your followers, then address the happiness problems in your team.
- ☐ Increase your self-confidence and that of your followers by mastering new skills and setting achievable goals so people can "win".

Now let's explore "Doc"trine #2 and uncover Profit Stealers TM that could be costing you money—and happiness.

"DOC"TRINE #2: BE SOMEONE WORTH FOLLOWING

Would you follow you?

The Payoff

You're a role model for your followers, and you inspire them to do great things in your business and beyond (even though you're still imperfect).

"Doc"trine #2 in Action: The Metamorphosis

When I first met Frank he was a partner in a struggling professional services firm. Bright and hardworking, he was a successful business developer. Unfortunately, he had a blind spot the size of Wyoming—his people-skills were fatally flawed. When winning over prospects and working with clients, he was adept at relating upward, but terrible at relating sideways and downward with his peers and subordinates. In these relationships, he was perfectionistic, critical, and domineering.

Needless to say, Frank didn't make a good partner or supervisor. His co-workers tolerated him because of his ability to bring in business, but within the firm he regularly destroyed morale and motivation. Some of the most talented people began leaving the business, and Frank was responsible for this exodus.

The managing partner and I decided we needed either to fire Frank or ask him to change his ways. Candidly, I was leaning toward firing him because he hadn't shown any willingness to acknowledge his serious shortcomings, much less address them. Concerned that Frank would continue to damage the firm's performance, I spoke with him privately about "opportunities" to change, but his response was less than enthusiastic.

Soon after in one of our regular partner planning meetings, he decided he wanted to talk about this issue. To say he was incensed is an understatement. With his face red and teeth clenched, he said, "Saying that I'm not good with people is an insult to me as a partner in this firm and as a man!"

Some tense discussion followed, but that was the beginning of the *most dramatic personal transformation I have ever witnessed!*

Frank asked me to help him take his leadership skills to the next level, so we set up a long-overdue coaching plan for him. In addition, he asked for regular feedback from his peers and his subordinates, and he pursued additional training on his own. The net result: Frank improved his skills dramatically and quickly. Because of his incredible positive metamorphosis, within a year he was promoted to president of the firm. Boy, were we glad we didn't fire him…

Good leaders are good parents

All organizations are based on the design and dynamics of the nuclear family. Therefore, because of the huge difference in power between the two, the relationship between leaders and followers is very similar in nature to the relationship between parents and children.

As an aside, please don't send me hate mail because I'm comparing followers to children. In the last chapter, I talked about the reality that we're all like children at heart. Besides, I'm not claiming followers are children; I'm only saying their situation is similar from the perspective of power dynamics.

Realistically, when we choose to work for someone else, we turn over some of our decision-making power and autonomy to that leader. We do that regularly, and it's impossible to be the top decision maker in every aspect of our lives. For example, if you were having surgery, would you want the surgeon to wake you up and ask for your leadership on how to proceed?

To get the best response from followers, a leader needs to do the same five things for a business that a good parent does for a family:

1. Safeguard the welfare of the entire family/business
2. Clarify the culture, goals, and core values
3. Make sure the members know the leader cares about them
4. Support the members in achieving their personal goals
5. Hold the members accountable for behaving in ways that are good for the welfare of the whole family/business

Remember Frank from our case study above? He wasn't behaving like a good parent. In fact, he was behaving like an abusive father. His employee "kids" were so afraid of him that many started to run away from home!

High-performance habit: Always care about your employee "kids," but hold them accountable to do what's best for the whole business "family."

The only real limitation on your business is YOU

The only *real* limitations on the success of any business are the weaknesses of its leader. Sure, people change, markets change, and economies change, but good leaders also change and adapt to make sure their businesses continue to be as successful as they want them to be.

This is The Leader Trickle Down Law SM. Leaders' personalities will "trickle down" through their organizations because they have so much more power than their followers. In other words, leaders' personalities become the personalities of their businesses. The behaviors they value and reward continue, and those that they dislike or punish go away, along with the employees who don't like this "culture." As a result, the strengths and weaknesses of the leader become the strengths and weaknesses of the business (see figure below).

LEADER TRICKLE-DOWN LAW

A business takes on the personality of its leader

Our case study of Frank demonstrates that his weaknesses of perfectionism and an overblown need to dominate others hurt his business. He created poor employee morale and motivation and lost productivity and profit. Once he addressed these weaknesses, however, his business immediately showed better results.

High-performance habit: Be the best leader you can be—your weaknesses become your business' weaknesses.

Honor the power of the truth

The truth really will set you free. People and computers are alike in one important way: If you put garbage in, you get garbage out. This means that the quality of human output is only as good as the quality of the input. If everyone in your team is sitting around talking BS, meaning giving inaccurate information, then you can be assured your business will get BS results.

I've worked with numerous teams in which it was more important to protect the leader's oversized ego than it was to tell the truth about what was and wasn't working in the business. As a leader you have the power to create a business culture in which it is safe to tell the truth, because you control the rewards and punishments in that environment.

The *best* way to create a culture of honesty is to model it yourself. Specifically, send a clear message that you value the truth by regularly seeking and accepting feedback. You don't always need to act on the feedback; listening and caring are the most important elements in the interactions. Make sure everyone knows that you value accurate information far more than protecting your ego from damaging an imagined standard of "perfection" you're holding yourself to.

High-performance habit: Don't run from the truth—it's faster than you.

Lead by example

Integrity is one of the most important values you can model. It's one of the essential ingredients of trust, and people worth having on your team won't follow a leader without integrity. If you tell your team not to pad their expense accounts, but you do, don't be surprised if dishonesty shows up in other ways in your business. It's all in the spirit of: Your behavior is so loud that I can't hear what you're saying.

Stephen Covey (1992) pointed out the difference between the "character ethic" and the "personality ethic." The character ethic holds that people succeed in life based on their character (e.g., having integrity). On the other hand, the "personality ethic" holds that people succeed by using shortcuts, such as manipulating situations to get what they want (e.g., some sales training techniques).

In my experience, we can't find a valid substitute for character in successful leadership. People want to follow someone they can respect, trust, and admire, and manipulative people don't fit these criteria. Our friend Frank above was a terrible exemplar for his followers. Do you think he really wanted everyone in his business to be overly critical and domineering? Not likely.

The trust-profit connection

Trust has two major components:

1. **Reliability:** Doing what you say you'll do, and
2. **Consideration:** Caring about the other person

When you say you trust particular individuals, you usually mean that they are reliable (do what they say they'll do) and that they care about you. Heck, you could trust Attila the Hun to rape and pillage (reliable), but most folks wouldn't use trust that way (not particularly caring).

Sustained business success is dependent upon good relationships, and good relationships are impossible without trust. So the causal chain looks like this:

THE TRUST-PERFORMANCE CONNECTION

Decreased ambiguity/Increased consideration

⇩

Trust

⇩

Teamwork

⇩

Performance

Being reliable and considerate/caring leads to:

1.   Trust, which leads to
2.   Teamwork, which leads to
3.   Greater productivity, which leads to
4.   Greater profits and success.

In our case study, Frank was reliable, but he wasn't considerate. Therefore, his followers couldn't trust him, and teamwork, productivity, and profits suffered.

High-performance habit: Be reliable, considerate, and authentic if you want your followers to trust you.

Blind spots? What blind spots?

You likely know this story about the man who left a bar and walked to his car. As he approached a streetlight he saw another man, obviously inebriated, bent over looking intently at the ground.

"What are you looking for?" the man asked the drunk.

Slurring his words, the drunk said, "I'm looking for my car keys."

"Perhaps I can help," the man said. "Is this where you think you lost them?"

"No," the drunk replied, "but this is where the light is."

Don't we all tend to favor our familiar patterns of behavior, and in the process miss the opportunities we can't see? We don't know what we don't know. My favorite mentor said it this way: When it comes to our own behavior, all of a sudden we have the worst seat in the house.

Joe Luft and Harry Ingham created a model of this phenomenon, called the Johari Window (Joe and Harry, get it?) shown in the figure below:

THE JOHARI WINDOW

	Known to self	Unknown to self
Known to others	OPEN	BLIND SPOT
Unknown to others	HIDDEN	UNKNOWN

As you can see, there are several factors at work. We don't know some things about ourselves, but we have a choice about whether we share what we do know about ourselves with others. We can choose to be open or we can choose to hide what we know. Meanwhile, others can see some things about us that we don't; those are our blind spots.

Think about it. Others evaluate our behavior based on our behavior. For example, if we mistreat someone, then our friends will figure that we're likely to mistreat them as well. However, we tend to evaluate our own behavior through the lens of our emotions and intentions. "Well, he was a jerk, so I had a right to mistreat him." Sometimes we rationalize some very bad decisions this way.

I once worked with Seth, the President of a large manufacturing company, who was one of the brightest and most progressive leaders I've ever known. However, there was a running joke among the vice presidents that he changed his mind about things constantly depending upon whom he'd talked with most recently. They even created an acronym to describe this phenomenon: LOWS (Last One With Seth). Once we made him aware of this blind spot, he changed his approach to provide a more stable and consistent direction for his team.

Inevitably, others hold us accountable for our behavior, but often they don't know what drives us. Regardless of what we're thinking and feeling, shouldn't we also hold ourselves accountable for our behavior?

We all have blind spots, but the fewer we have, the more likely we are to make better choices that help us be happy and successful. Therefore, blind spots are not your friends. Here are two powerful ways to eliminate blind spots:

1. Seek situations where you're likely to hear new perspectives on important areas, such as training, mentoring, coaching, and candid peer groups.
2. Ask for feedback. Leaders who seek feedback become more successful over time; leaders who don't look for feedback become less successful over time.

Fortunately, we don't even have to act on the feedback, but can choose to if we see a clear advantage in it. Either way, it's almost always better to know than not know.

Our friend Frank certainly didn't consciously want to be a mean person who undermined his own happiness and success, but because of his blind spots he managed to do just that. To his credit, once he became aware of his blind spots he addressed them decisively and courageously and reaped the rewards of his efforts.

High-performance habit: Eliminate your blind spots.

Beware of Profit Stealers ™

Some blind spots are costlier than others. Some of the worst offenders are unrealistic fears, which I call Profit Stealers TM. Profit Stealers TM are blind spots that cost you a lot of money. Some of the worst Profit Stealers include these often repeated and generally accepted guidelines or principles, plus their counterpoints:

1. We must set "stretch" goals that no one can be optimistic about achieving. (Usually, people get discouraged and quit trying.)
2. Caring about others shows weakness. (Caring/consideration is the #1 predictor of leadership success or failure.)
3. The leader needs to be the "smartest person in the room." (You'll have an awfully weak team if you have to be the best at everything.)
4. My employees are lazy and don't care about my business. (Either you're hiring the wrong people or not giving them a reason to care.)
5. I must never show weakness or indecision. (Being authentic when

you don't have the answers encourages others to do the same.)

Frank's fears of being "not good enough" drove him to do some self-destructive things in his business. Once he put these fears to rest and replaced them with realistic expectations, he began to flourish as a leader.

High-performance habit: Address your personal insecurities so they don't hurt your business.

High-Performance Habits Checklist

- ☐ Always care about your employee "kids," but hold them accountable to do what's best for the whole business "family."
- ☐ Be the best leader you can be—the only real limitations on your business success are your weaknesses.
- ☐ Don't run from the truth—it's faster than you.
- ☐ If you want your followers to trust you, be reliable, considerate, and authentic.
- ☐ Eliminate your blind spots.
- ☐ Address your personal insecurities so they don't hurt your business success.

In "Doc"trine #3, we'll continue to work on leadership skills, with an emphasis on working smarter, not harder (which is a lot more fun and profitable!).

"DOC"TRINE #3: FOCUS YOUR VISION

Stop making glacial progress on a thousand different fronts and focus.

The Payoff

You and your team are excited, mobilized, and motivated around a clear and focused vision for your business (and thank goodness you don't have to try to be "all things to all people" anymore).

"Doc"trine #3 in Action: Glaciers Are Big and Slow

While working as part of a consulting team with a major manufacturing company, I asked one of the leaders at the plant how things were going. Without missing a beat, he smiled sardonically and said, "We're making glacial progress on a thousand different fronts."

The CEO, Charles, was an ambitious leader and a progressive thinker who was famous for being unafraid to try new things. He was also famous, however, for playing fast and loose with the company's money; so much so that he'd earned the nickname "Charlie Coin." He had costly new initiatives going on all over the corporation, and his leadership team complained that they had so many meetings to keep track of all this that they literally had no time to tend to the core business operations.

Despite our best efforts, we couldn't get the CEO to focus his vision to include fewer, more manageable goals (and pay more attention to cash flow). In fact, as money got tighter our consulting team was dismissed to save cost, so we lost any influence we might have had in helping determine the future direction of the company. The company was out of business within two years.

Don't waste your organizational energy

In the figure below you can see the human energy involved in a business conceptualized in a graphic.

*YOUR BUSINESS' ENERGY SYSTEM*_℠

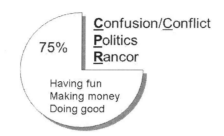

25% wasted time & money

If 100% of the energy of the people in the business was focused on being happy, making money, and doing good, the business would hum along spectacularly. In most businesses, however, a good portion of the human energy gets siphoned off in confusion about the goals, roles, and values. This leads to conflict, politics, and rancor (a fancy word for unhappiness).

In this situation, the organization needs CPR (cardiopulmonary resuscitation)! Clarifying the goals, roles, and values, however, can focus the business' energy back on being happy, making money, and doing good—and the profits will show it. In our manufacturing company case study, there was confusion about too many goals and unclear priorities, which lead to political wrangling and a great deal of conflict over money resources behind the scenes (rancor).

High-performance habit: Create a clear and focused business vision to be happy, make money, and do good (by providing a valuable service in the marketplace).

You need an effective strategy and effective tactics

Remember that strategy and leadership are about what, and tactics and management are about how. In other words, tactics are about "doing things right," whereas strategy is about "doing the right things" (Drucker, 2001). Of course we want to have both a great strategy and great tactical implementation of that strategy.

It seems to be part of the human condition that when all is said and done, a lot more is said than done. In any strategy meeting, we will consider many different objectives and alternatives to achieve those objectives, but will ultimately narrow all this down to a clear achievable strategy and tactics. To repeat, a strategy must be sound and its tactics must be implemented well in order to enjoy sustained success.

In our case study for this chapter, the manufacturing company's overall strategy appeared to be "industry innovation leader," but its overall tactics seemed to be "change everything at once" without any regard to running out of money before the changes could create profit.

EFFECTIVE STRATEGY & TACTICS

	Unclear	Clear
Effective	- Unclear strategy + Effective tactics (3)	+ Clear strategy + Effective tactics (1)
Tactics (How)	- Unclear strategy - Ineffective tactics (4)	+ Clear strategy - Ineffective tactics (2)
Ineffective		

Unclear   **Strategy (What)**   Clear

High-performance habit: Create a focused, achievable strategy and effective implementation tactics.

"Embrace" the revised KISS Principle

I'm a huge fan of the revised KISS Principle: Keep It Simple and Short (the KISS Principle, only shorter). In my experience, the more complex things are, the less likely anything will get done.

Take vision statements, for example. Many business owners put everything but the kitchen sink into their vision statements. These long statements tend to mix vision, mission, and values, along with every flowery extraneous adjective they can think of. These visions can run half a page, and by the time you get to the end you've forgotten what it said in the beginning. For example, "Our vision is to end world hunger by working really hard and loving our mothers as we put together a marketing plan that is essentially a social media platform that etc., etc., etc. ..." You get the idea.

The overriding point is to focus on where you're headed, and express it in a way that's easily understood and communicated to your stakeholder groups (e.g., your team, customers, and prospective employees). Everyone on your team should be able to tell you what the vision is without hesitation, and you certainly can't do that with a long, unwieldy vision statement.

One of the best vision statements I ever played a role in creating was written for a water heater manufacturing company: "To be the world's largest provider of hot water products and services."

High-performance habit: Keep all your plans simple and communicable so they'll get implemented.

Focus on what's really important to your success

Bill Cosby famously said, "I don't know the key to success, but the key to failure is trying to please everybody." Insufficient focus is the most frequent mistake in strategic planning and its subsequent implementation. It's difficult for most of us to avoid the temptation to be all things to all people, or to pursue business opportunities that seem "nice to do" but end up leading us to do too much with too few resources. We forget that by saying yes to some opportunities, we by necessity say no to others. The trick is to make these choices consciously through good planning, rather than haphazardly through doing everything that seems nice to do. Remember the steel mill story at the beginning of this chapter?

We'll always see more good ideas and opportunities than we have resources (i.e., time and money) to pursue. We wind up not only saying no to the bad ideas, but we must say no to a lot of good ideas as well. A clear vision informs these day-to-day decision-making priorities.

In the U.S. we're obsessively caught up in the "work ethic." We're so busy "working hard" that we fail to place enough emphasis on "working smart." Achieving results is a much better measure of success than effort expended, and no amount of "heroic" effort can replace good planning and execution.

This comes down to education and training, which explains why businesses that maintain financial success over a sustained period tend to emphasize training and development. When done well, this is an investment with a great return on investment.

For example, the leading producer—by far—in the sales department was being criticized by his peers for spending too much time on the golf course with his clients and potential clients and not enough time at "work." However, as the sales manager said, "Perhaps the rest of us would be well advised to spend more time playing golf!"

Franklin-Covey (Covey, 1994) has a helpful planning and execution tool called The Law of Diminishing Returns. Their research found that businesses who have:

- 2-3 strategic goals usually achieve all of them
- 4-10 strategic goals usually achieve 1-2 of them
- 11-20 strategic goals usually achieve none of them

Our manufacturing company CEO at the beginning of the chapter comes to mind. Making glacial progress on a thousand different fronts didn't serve him well at all.

My favorite time management tool is Stephen Covey's "Urgent versus Important" matrix (1994, see figure below).

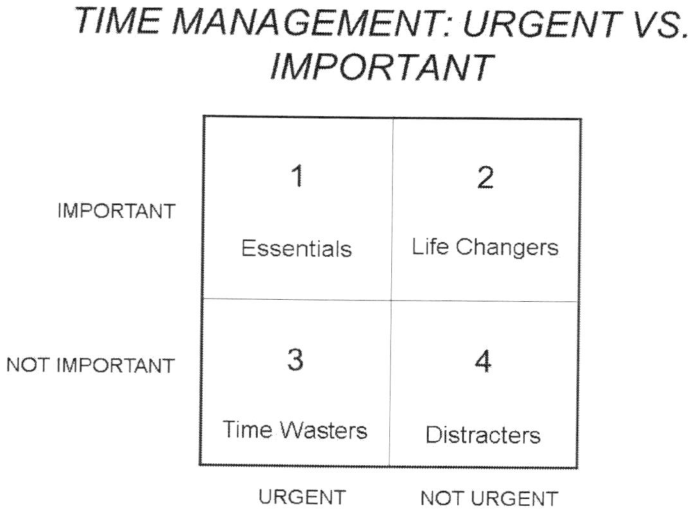

TIME MANAGEMENT: URGENT VS. IMPORTANT

	URGENT	NOT URGENT
IMPORTANT	**1** Essentials	**2** Life Changers
NOT IMPORTANT	**3** Time Wasters	**4** Distracters

You'll always get the tasks done in quadrant 1, which are both urgent and important. If an important customer has an important need, for example, you'll find a way to meet it. Most folks recognize that tasks falling into quadrant 4 (not urgent and not important) aren't worth the effort. If a vendor is trying to get an appointment with you to sell a new sales training system when your sales department is doing great, you aren't likely to grant the appointment.

The real opportunities for happiness and success lie in quadrants 3 and 2. A lot of our time is eaten up by activities that seem urgent but aren't important to our success. For example, superfluous email can take up hours of your days and weeks without leading to any real payoff.

If you create the discipline to ignore the siren call of that kind of busy work, you'll free up time to focus on things important to the success of your business but not urgent in the sense of being due tomorrow. For example, strategic planning is essential to your long-term success, but typically nothing disastrous will occur tomorrow if you put it off. Here's the rub: If you let enough tomorrows pass, the disaster inevitably comes. In that same vein, it takes great effort to put in processes to insure that you're hiring the best people, so it's easy to put off the work of designing those processes. If you put it off long enough, however, bad things surely happen because the quality of your team deteriorates over time. The takeaway here is to decrease your busy work and make time for the things that are important to the long term success of your business.

High-performance habit: Focus on the few goals that are truly important to your success.

Set achievable goals so you can "win"

In some quarters, it's apparently popular to set goals that are euphemistically called "stretch goals." Don't get me wrong; I'm all for Big Hairy Audacious Goals that get everyone thinking big picture and becoming excited about the possibilities of what the team can achieve.

However, we like to win, and we lose motivation if we're always falling short of unattainable goals. At that point, the goal itself begins to create negative feelings. Most of us start to resent the goal and even treat it as a joke and an indication of how unreasonable, out of touch, and inept the leader is.

As you can see from the figure below, the relationship between goal/standard setting and performance matches the typical bell curve, with a fairly broad optimum range for goal/standard setting that gets the best from your team. Setting goals at either extreme (too low or too high) leaves performance on the table.

FOR MAXIMUM PERFORMANCE:
LOWER YOUR STANDARDS

Performance

Mediocrity   Excellence   Perfection

Performance standard

The leaders I advise are high achievers, and high achievers often lean toward perfectionism, and sometimes they want to set the performance standard for their teams as "perfect." I often have a tough time talking them into setting the performance standard as "excellence" instead.

For starters, perfection is an abstract concept. We can easily apply it to sunsets on Oahu, Hawaii, but not so much to human endeavors. The extra energy expended, ensuing frustration, and diminished motivation resulting from failed efforts to achieve perfection simply waste human effort. Our case study manufacturing company CEO set the bar at "perfection" because he refused to acknowledge that all the changes he envisioned couldn't be achieved overnight, and he got the results you'd expect.

To be fair, going too far in the other direction doesn't achieve the best results either. Setting the performance bar at "mediocrity" leaves the members of your team feeling unchallenged and apathetic (e.g., my experience is that many of the employees of the U.S. Postal Service aren't particularly concerned about excellent customer service).

High-performance habit: Set achievable goals so your team can "win" and your business can succeed.

What kind of car is your business?

If your business were a car, what kind of car would it be? For example, would you be a Porsche Carrera (high performance, high price), a Honda Accord (high quality, moderate price), or a Chevrolet Nova (moderate quality, low price)? How you structure your business makes a big difference.

For example, my local Porsche dealership is the Taj Mahal of car dealerships, right down to a latte and snack bar in the customer waiting area. You can't walk into the place without being covered up with service, and they price everything as though it's all made of gold. Our Honda dealership is a lot less high-end but eminently more affordable. Given the average budget, the lack of gold-plated services is often worth it for a more affordable car.

It's next to impossible to pull off being the highest quality product with the lowest price in your market, so don't even go there. Decide what kind of car you are, and build your "dealership" accordingly.

High-performance habit: Decide how you want to position your business in the marketplace, and then be consistent in your communications to that market.

A way to inspire creative visioning

Before writing your vision statement, try some brainstorming exercises to get your planning team thinking broadly and out of the box. Otherwise, you'll likely find those involved will think in an incremental and evolutionary way about your business strategy, and you might overlook a revolutionary new idea that could be highly successful and profitable.

First, conduct a SWOT Analysis. We'll talk about this tool in more detail in Chapter 8, "Measure Success," but essentially the acronym SWOT stands for Strengths, Weaknesses, Opportunities, and Threats. The idea is to identify the most important internal strengths (e.g., strong personnel), internal weaknesses (e.g., insufficient teamwork), external opportunities (e.g., new untapped market), and external threats (e.g., new competitor in your niche) for your business currently.

Then brainstorm at least one potential action you could take for every entry in the analysis. For example, if one of your greatest external opportunities is "strategic partnership with the ABC Company," then one potential action might be to set up a meeting with the ABC Company CEO to discuss this idea. For more detail on how to brainstorm effectively, see Chapter 12, "Institutionalize Innovation."

How to write a vision statement

I have seen vision statements written many ways, but I prefer one that includes:

1. Where do we want to go in our planning horizon (usually 3-5 years)?
2. By when?

A vision statement should be:

1. Exciting and motivating to those in the business
2. Realistically achievable

For example, "We will be the largest provider of wealth management services in the United States by March 31, 2017," or "We will win the award for the best beet producers' professional association by October 1, 2018."

Imagine a headline in a significant news publication, such as *The New York Times, The Wall Street Journal,* or an online news source, at the end of your strategic planning horizon, let's say, three years. What would you like the headline to read on that day? For example, it could say, "The ACME Company Achieves a Dominant World Market Share in Anvil Sales!" or "The Mr. Green Jeans Company Voted Greenest Business in the USA!" This exercise helps you clarify your vision of "what you want to be when you grow up."

Can your business boat sail in a Blue Ocean for a while?

At its most basic and simple, Blue Ocean Strategy (Mauborgne & Kim, 2005) is designed to create a business strategy in which you have no competitors. Instead of competing in the "bloody red ocean" where many businesses vie for market share, you create a "blue ocean" new market in which you have no competitors. For example, this might be a new product altogether, or it could be tapping new markets or distribution channels for an existing product.

For example, when Apple first introduced the iPhone, it was a product so different from anything else on the market that for a time Apple had no competitors for it. Competitors inevitably will encroach on any "blue ocean" business strategy, however, and then it's time to seek another "blue ocean."

How to write a mission statement

Again, dispense with the "everything but the kitchen sink" approach and keep it simple and understandable. The three main components are:

1. What products/services do we provide?
2. For whom?
3. Where?

For example: "We manufacture anvils for big box retailers in the United States," or "We provide comprehensive coordination of marathon races worldwide."

Depending upon the complexity of your business, you may need to write more than one mission statement for different customer segments or markets. In fact, it's useful to have every individual and existing work group in your business craft a mission statement. Everyone in the business provides something for someone somewhere, and we all have customers that we need to please in order to succeed.

For example, for the anvil manufacturer above, the mission of its human resources department might be, "We attract and retain the best employees so our company can manufacture anvils for big box retailers in the United States," or the mission statement of the marketing department might be "We create interest among potential buyers for our anvils so big box retailers can sell more of them."

High-performance habit: Write clear and simple vision and mission statements for your business, and make sure all your employees know what they are.

How to stand out from your competitors

Why will people buy from you instead of your competition? The Star Model (Haines, 2007) of value positioning is a useful tool for this purpose. In this model, the five major points of business differentiation are:

1. Personal choice/customization (e.g., Lillian Vernon, Tesla)
2. Caring service (e.g., Zappos, Nordstrom's)
3. High quality (e.g., Lexus, Apple)
4. Total cost (e.g., WalMart, Costco)
5. Delivery responsiveness (Federal Express, Domino's)

Although a business must be reasonably competent at all these value points, we're wise to focus on one of them in order to show that we're different enough to truly to differentiate ourselves from our competitors.

High-performance habit: Decide how you will make your business stand out so potential customers will buy from you instead of your competitors.

Create the Strategic Priorities for your vision

Once you have created a clear vision, it's time to create your Strategic Priorities, but no more than three to five or they cease being priorities and become a "to do" list.

To create these Strategic Priorities, ask the question: "What initiatives must we absolutely accomplish to achieve our vision?" One of your Strategic Priorities might be, "Hire a new COO," or "Increase marketing effectiveness," or "Improve customer satisfaction." Then you can set a specific measurable target for the priority, such as, "Hire a new COO by March 16."

High-performance habit: Focus your resources (time and money) on three to five Strategic Priorities that MUST be accomplished in order to achieve your vision.

Decide on your Priority Actions for this year

For each Strategic Priority, decide on three or fewer Priority Actions for the current year. If one of your Strategic Priorities is "Increase sales," then one of your Priority Actions for this year could be, "Hire a new salesperson by September 15." See Chapter 8, "Measure It (Size Matters)," for more detail on how to measure and track Strategic Priorities and Priority Actions.

The SMART model (Doran, 1981) is an effective tool for creating reachable goals. SMART goals are:

- Specific
- Measurable
- Attainable
- Relevant
- Time bound

For example, "John (accountable person) will increase his gross sales number (specific and measurable) by 20% (attainable) by June 30 (time bound)." We're assuming the goal is relevant to John's success and to the success of the business. SMART goals remove the ambiguity in some goal-setting exercises that leads to poor execution.

High-performance habit: Focus your resources (time and money) on three or fewer Priority Actions for each strategic priority for the coming year.

High-performance habit: Create SMART goals (specific, measurable, achievable, relevant, time bound).

High-Performance Habits Checklist

- ☐ Create a clear and focused business vision to be happy, make money, and do good (by providing a valuable service in the marketplace).
- ☐ Create a focused, achievable strategy and effective implementation tactics.
- ☐ Keep all your plans simple and communicable so they'll get implemented.
- ☐ Focus on the few goals that are truly important to your success.
- ☐ Set achievable goals so your team can "win" and your business can succeed.
- ☐ Decide how you want to position your business in the marketplace, and then be consistent in your communications with that market.
- ☐ Decide how you will make your business stand out so potential customers will buy from you instead of your competitors.
- ☐ Write clear and simple vision and mission statements for your business, and make sure all your employees know what they are.
- ☐ Focus your resources (time and money) on three to five Strategic Priorities that MUST be accomplished in order to achieve your vision.
- ☐ Focus your resources (time and money) on three or fewer Priority Actions for each strategic priority for the coming year.
- ☐ High-performance habit: Create SMART goals (specific, measurable, achievable, relevant, time bound).

How do your core values affect your business? "Doc"trine #4 explores the differences in happiness and profit levels in businesses with a core value of "mutual respect" or "caring about others" versus "make a dollar however we can."

"DOC"TRINE #4: VALUE YOUR VALUES

You can't be a great leader without first being a great human being.

The Payoff

You're sleeping well at night because your team is getting great results while following the core values of your business (and you're not at all worried about "terrorists" in your organization).

"Doc"trine #4 in Action: The Terrorist

I worked with a professional services firm that had a bright young male associate who was creating a large revenue stream through his business development efforts. However, he and his young female assistant were having an extramarital affair. Both were married and had children. Despite my recommendations to the contrary, the partners hadn't intervened in this situation because the associate was making so much money for the firm.

In a strategic planning meeting, I asked the partners what they intended to do about this development, which was adversely affecting the atmosphere in their firm. The affair was an open secret, and made for juicy water cooler gossip. The message the firm's silence sent to the staff reflected the core values of the business: "It's okay to lie and cheat as long as you don't get caught."

The managing partner simply said, "Well Terry, we're not going to do anything about it, because this kid is golden."

You see it coming, don't you?

One day, the assistant's husband showed up at the firm waving a pistol and threatening to kill this golden kid.

After the lawsuits flew, the press raged, and the dust settled, the firm had lost far more money, morale, and motivation than they ever enjoyed from the associate's initial financial success. No one was happy, making money, or doing the most good in this situation.

Clear core values form a solid foundation for trusting relationships

It's important to look at the way you get results in your business. Making your fortune by mistreating others is not a sustainable business model, because business is about relationships, whether face-to-face or virtual. As an approach to business, mistreating others (partners, customers, or employees) may work for the short term, at least until people realize that they're being treated badly, but in a free society, it will never work in the long term.

Most people won't stick around for a relationship after they've been mistreated. We can see a huge difference in how employees and customers respond to a business with a core value of "mutual respect" or "caring about others" versus "make a dollar however we can."
Don't you feel this way? Do you do business with people who don't care about you or are out to mistreat you?

Clear core values are critical to your business. These values define "how we do things around here." True, core values may sometimes get a bad rap of being all "mom and apple pie." However, that negative talk comes up only when the business or individual doesn't adhere to its stated core values. We don't have to look far to see examples of what the "let's do whatever it takes to make a buck" approach yields. Think Enron, Arthur Anderson Consulting, the subprime mortgage scandal, and so forth.

Living by constructive core values is essential to achieving your goals now and in the future. I mean, really, do you want financial success at the cost of doing things that lead you to feel bad about yourself or keep you awake at night? That's too high a price to pay, and it won't work long term anyway.

None of our potential customers want to do business with someone who is motivated mostly by money. That's called greed, and it's not good for sustained success (regardless of what Michael Douglas, aka Gordon Gekko, said in the movie Wall Street). Lack of adherence to solid core values (which typically don't include greed) is also what caused the partners in our case-study service firm above to use poor judgment in dealing with their two-timing associate. In the bargain, they lost a great deal of money and good will from both employees and clients.

Don't succumb to greed—it will kill sustained business success

Speaking of greed, everyone accepts that a business needs to make a profit in order to keep providing its services. What many leaders fail to understand, however, are the very real dangers of greed. Greed is essentially a displaced attempt to meet an emotional need for love and happiness (important to us all) by continuously accumulating more money, power, and status without concern for how this quest affects those around us. It's an endless appetite that can't be satisfied, because no amount of money, status, or power can meet the real need they attempt to fill.

Greed is a special case of imbalance as established by the Principle of Balance and Justification (PB&J) TM presented in Chapter 1.

Here's the causal chain as I see it:

1. Happiness is our most important goal in life.
2. Positive psychology teaches us that about all the happiness we'll get from our money occurs when we have enough to pay our bills and some left over to have some fun. In today's dollars, anything more than around $75K provides little or no incremental happiness.
3. What good is a preoccupation with making even more money once we have enough to be happy?
4. If money is the first business and life priority of the members of your team, without caring about the needs and happiness of others (greed), then your team will provide poor customer service.
5. Greedy team members will start to feed on each other and destroy overall teamwork, productivity, and profits.
6. If you start off being greedy, sooner or later you'll wind up bankrupt, both financially and emotionally.

You'll make more money by prioritizing people over money and happiness over achievement. At first blush this may sound counterintuitive. How can a for-profit business not focus first and foremost on achievement and money? What kind of malarkey is this?

This priority makes great sense, however, if you want sustained high performance in your business. It turns out that in order to achieve great things consistently over time men and women need to be happy and motivated from within. It also turns out that to make money consistently, we need other people (e.g., employees, customers). That means happiness and people are leading indicators, and achievement and money are lagging indicators. Therefore, it follows that if you make sure your employees are happy, they will achieve great things and make money, and you'll do good in the process by providing a great service to the marketplace.

The reverse is also true. If you prioritize achievement and money over happiness and people, then you may achieve some financial success in the short term, but your employees will cease performing in the long run. How can you have sustained achievement and financial success without happy and motivated people doing the work of the business?

High-performance habit: For sustained financial success, don't be greedy—prioritize happiness over achievement and people over money.

How to create effective core values for your business

I recommend you list no more than seven core values. Fewer are even better. If we name too many core values we diminish the impact of having the values in the first place. Keep the list simple and succinct, which allows them to be understood, communicated, and remembered easily.

I like using a one- or two-word phrase followed by a brief behavioral description. For example, the core values for our business are:

1. Happiness. We make the world a happier place.
2. Integrity. We do what we say we're going to do.
3. Success. We see financial success as important to happiness.

Can your followers tell you what the core values of your business are?

High-performance habit: Define three to seven clear, succinct core values for your business.

How to use core values to drive business results

You can use core values in the following four ways to:

1. Guide strategic and tactical decision making (e.g., asking the question: Does that fit within our strategy and our core values?)
2. Produce advertising materials (e.g., reflecting the belief: This is what we stand for. Wouldn't you like to do business with us?)
3. Develop recruiting materials (e.g., reflecting the belief: This is what we stand for. Wouldn't you like to be on our team?)
4. Guide your performance management system (e.g., stating the attitude: We value the fact that you display integrity and respect for others in all that you do.).

High-performance habit: Make your core values non-negotiable in your business, and use them to drive business results.

Get rid of "terrorists"

Jack Welch, the much-admired former leader of General Electric, had a simple system for evaluating the members of his business, as seen in the figure below.

THE JACK WELCH GRID

	"Cheerleaders" (Likely to take coaching)	"All Stars" ("A" players)
Values	"Dead Wood" (Bad hires)	"Terrorists" (Not likely to take coaching)
	Results	

Values appear on the vertical axis, and run from a high level of an individual's values match with the business at the top to a low level at the bottom. Results appear on the horizontal axis, and run from an individual's poor results on the left to great results on the right.

The best employees are those in the northeast quadrant; they get great results and have the right values (the All Stars, or "A" Players). The second best employees are those in the northwest quadrant; they have the right values (e.g., integrity, team orientation) but aren't getting great results (the Cheerleaders). These individuals usually need coaching and training to acquire the skills to get good results, and they're usually hungry for these experiences.

The people in the southwest quadrant aren't getting great results, and they don't have the right values (Dead Wood). They're bad hires—someone wasn't paying attention when they were brought on board and they're not a good fit for the business. You'd be wise to examine your hiring practices to identify flaws are that lead to bad hiring decisions.

The people in the southeast quadrant, the terrorists, get great results but have the wrong values; these individuals are the most dangerous people in your organization—they will destroy it from the inside out. They typically enjoy short-term financial success, but they're not particularly interested in training or coaching meant to change destructive behavior. People who have become financially successful tend to over generalize their success and begin to believe they know everything about everything. They often tune out information that doesn't fit within their exaggerated sense of power.

Get the terrorists out of your business regardless of the income stream they produce; you will *always* experience a net loss personally and professionally in the long term. Remember our case-study services firm? I bet they wish they had jettisoned their Terrorist before he created a situation that "blew up" and caused so much damage to the business!

High-performance habit: Get rid of Terrorist employees who don't live the core values of your business.

Decide if you want a religion-based business

If your passion is to build a business around a specific religion as your core values, then go all the way. Chick-Fil-A provides a good example of a business that has done well with this approach.

It's wise, however, to make this decision with your eyes wide open, keeping in mind the tradeoffs you're making. It really depends on your vision for the business. A specific religion-based business may not appeal to those whose religious orientation differs from yours. It's possible; perhaps even likely, you'll limit your potential customer base. In addition, be aware that if you bring in employees who don't share your religious beliefs, they could feel like outsiders and might find it challenging to integrate fully into the team. This carries the risk of limiting teamwork in your organization.

I have consulted with several companies who have wrestled with this issue, and ultimately it's important to come to a decision that is in concert with the vision of the business leader. Forming a religion-based business is a perfectly viable business strategy option. It's good to keep in mind that you'll never succeed in pleasing everybody anyway.

High-performance habit: If you decide on a religion-based business, understand how it will affect internal and external business considerations.

High-Performance Habits Checklist

☐ Define clear core values for your business, and make them non-negotiable.

☐ Use your core values to drive business results through performance management of existing employees, recruiting new employees, and marketing.

☐ For sustained financial success, don't be greedy—prioritize happiness over achievement and people over money.

☐ Get rid of Terrorist employees who don't live the core values of your business.

☐ If you decide on a religion-based business, understand how it will affect internal and external business considerations.

Would you like to spend a lot more time leading and a lot less time managing? Find out how in "Doc"trine #5 so you can start winning more often.

"DOC"TRINE #5: FIELD A PRO TEAM

When a pro team competes against a high school team, the outcome is a foregone conclusion.

The Payoff

You spend a lot more time leading and a lot less time managing. You win much more often than not (and you've realized you don't even have to be the smartest person in the room).

"Doc"trine #5 in Action: The Ultimate Pro Team

A professional services firm came to me with what they described as "a small turnover problem." They were prompted to act when their recently-hired receptionist fell through a glass coffee table in the reception area of their office. Really? This event made more sense when I discovered that the receptionist was an alcoholic who also had wrecked her car driving drunk to work that day. Do you think it was possible they were hiring the wrong people?

I worked with the leaders of the company for a number of years, and by the time they sold the business (and all walked away wealthy), we had nearly achieved our goal of having 90% "A" Players (those who were top 10% performers in their roles). The business oozed quality, with employees who were extremely good at their jobs and whose values were in line with the collaborative and entrepreneurial culture we had built.

The founder and majority owner was bright, ambitious, and charismatic, as well as a great marketer and public speaker. However, she tended toward perfectionism and was a much stronger leader than manager. Because of her perfectionism, she tended to be too harsh with her employees. In addition, she had an underused COO in the leadership team who was excellent at managing people and running the day-to-day business.

We persuaded the founder to focus her efforts on strategy, marketing, and sales and empowered the COO to run the day-to-day business, including managing most of the employees. We determined in what roles individuals could be "A" Players, and then we "let 'em play."

In addition, as the business flourished and we added new people to the team, we set up a thorough selection process that included my conducting an intensive individual assessment of potential new employees' skills and values before they were cleared to be hired. When the founder sold the business some years later, it commanded an impressive price, due in no small part to the caliber of the personnel on board.

If you want to win, field a pro team

Even if you're not a sports fan, indulge me for a minute. Since I'm in the U.S., let's talk American football (or basketball, or baseball—whatever sport you like best). The "A" Players (top 10% performers in their roles) in the game of football are the professional players, right? You have to be exceptional, at least in the top 10% of performers, to go pro in the National Football League. The "B" Players (well above average performers) are the college players. You have to be pretty darned good to play football at the college level. The "C" Players (average performers) are high school football players. Even these football players must possess a fairly impressive combination of size, strength, and speed to make a varsity high school football team.

Now imagine that you make your living as a professional gambler, which you *are* if you're an entrepreneur. This means that if you don't win your bets, your family goes hungry. You hear that for some crazy reason there's going to be a high-stakes game between your local NFL team and the state champion high school football team. Who would you bet on to win the game? What would the odds be? It's a pretty easy decision, eh?

Then why do so many leaders rationalize putting together a high school team and sending them out to compete against the pros? They might as well prepare for a massacre. And for goodness sake, please don't ask your quarterback to play center...

Success builds on success. Why would All Stars want to be on a team with a lot of average "C" players? If they did, they'd have control-freak issues in which they have to be the "big dog" all the time, which would make them not "A" Players anyway, right?

The benefits of having "A" Players in your team include:

1. High morale
2. High teamwork
3. High employee retention
4. High financial performance
5. Easy succession planning
6. Sustained competitive advantage
7. Sustained success

High-performance habit: Create a business with 90% "A" Players and "A" Player Potentials.

Feed your eagles

Derek Newton (1994) wrote *Feed Your Eagles*, a book about building high-performance sales teams. In it, he calls for spending your time and money on the high performers who will bring the greatest success to your business. I have seen untold time and money invested in trying to upgrade D Players to C Players through management, training, and coaching. Instead, invest your time and money in A Players and A Player Potentials who will help everyone in your business succeed, including you.

Business is a competitive game, with real winners and losers. Don't spend an undue amount of time and money trying to "rescue" chronically poor performing employees. (By the way, these folks are quite different from someone who is just going through a temporary rough patch of some sort). You unwittingly can become an enabler who makes it possible for poor performers to stay in roles in which they chronically underachieve and will never truly be happy. It's better for all concerned if you "free up their futures," so to speak, and allow them to find true happiness and success in another situation. Their happiness and success is not your responsibility—it is theirs.

We faced several critical decision points on the way to building our case-study pro team at the first of this chapter. At the beginning of the process, as we evaluated the talent we had on the team, we realized there were several team members in key roles that were not performing up to the standards we had set for the business. We first evaluated whether these team members were good candidates for coaching, and then provided this coaching when we thought we had a reasonable chance of upgrading the person's performance to an acceptable level. In several cases, however, the best thing for the business "family" was to part ways with an underperforming employee. These moves paid off handsomely in business performance later on.

In addition, there were some impressive success-stories among the "underperformers" that were let go. One equity holder formed his own firm and was very successful providing a considerably different valuable service to a different target market. Clearly, he was an "A" Player in his new business. I'm certain he would have said he was happier, making more money, and doing more good than before.

High-performance habit: Spend most of your time and money helping your "A" Players make your business more successful rather than "fixing" underperformers.

How to identify "A" Players

This discussion relates to the Jack Welch Grid, including A Players, in Chapter 4. Essentially, to be an A Player someone must:

1. Have values to match those of your business, and
2. Get exceptional results

Remember that someone may be a C Player in one role and an A Player in another, so get the right people into the right roles.

It's as easy as PIES ™

When we're looking for an A Player to fill a position, at a minimum we look for:

- **P**assion for the position: we want someone who is darned excited to be there!
- **I**ntelligence: intelligent people get more work done in less time.
- **E**motional intelligence: an understanding of people is paramount to successfully work in a team environment.
- **S**kills: either have the skills we need or can be trained in a reasonable amount of time.

It's worth noting that the single best predictor of achievement is raw general intelligence. Think about it—a more intelligent person will get more work done in the same amount of time. If you're not testing for intelligence as part of your hiring process, it's time to start.

Recognize the Three Levels of Achievers ™

Basically there are three levels of achievers in the world:

1. **Low achievers: Lazy people**. I don't like the "lazy" label, because I don't think it contributes much to understanding why a person isn't motivated to achieve. It's a little too convenient to call someone lazy and attribute lack of motivation to some internal personality flaw. This can be present, but I've seen too many good people called lazy when they were actually in an environment that did not motivate them to achieve. Ask yourself, "Have I given my followers a reason to care about my business?" If you're paying

them by the hour and micromanaging them, then probably not. As a result, these people don't achieve very much.

While I'm not opposed to unions in principle, many of the union employees I've worked with seem to fit this profile. They're paid by the hour, and they're distrusted and micromanaged. Therefore it doesn't make much sense for them to care about the whole enterprise. What's in it for them? Of course, if you truly have a follower who isn't motivated to pursue the goals of your business, then you have a clear mandate to "free up his future" so he can succeed elsewhere.

2. **Moderate achievers: Work ethic people.** These people achieve out of a fear of disapproval and punishment. Someone told them that to be a good person they need to work hard, which seems to mean "work until you are uncomfortable and unhappy." This stems from the Puritan religious tradition that celebrates work for work's sake (and at one point, for survival), and it's based on a black-and-white mentality, "good" versus "bad." Lord help us. These individuals tend to achieve a great deal because fear is a powerful motivator, but fear has its limitations. If overplayed, this approach can lead to obsessive behavior in which people are more focused on "working hard" than on "working smart" and getting results. Their end goal is to stay busy to avoid looking slothful, rather than achieving meaningful goals. If you still harbor a belief in the old saying, "Idle hands are the devil's workshop," then I invite you to reconsider that belief. People often need idle time to think of creative ways to take the business to the next level of performance. Some very successful companies specifically give employees idle time for this purpose (e.g., Google, Apple).

3. **High achievers: Passionate people**. People who are passionate about what they're doing will achieve the most of the three groups. Energetic and creative, they enjoy what they're doing. Over the long term, their passion for their work is a more powerful motivator than work ethic or a fear of being punished. Their focus on enjoying life and achieving meaningful results is the premium grade among fuels for achievers.

In hiring people for our case-study pro team, we were very deliberate in choosing employees who were passionate about the role we were filling. One specific example was the receptionist. We decided we wanted the best receptionist in town, so we identified the person we wanted and lured her away from a competitor.

Beware of "energy vampires"

"Energy vampires" are those folks who are basically unhappy and bring negative energy to your business. If you recall our discussion of your business as an energy system in Chapter 1, then you know that each team member in your business adds either happy, positive energy or unhappy, negative energy to the team.

Keep in mind that no one can be happy all the time—a Pollyanna—but we all have a fundamental happiness set point. Make it a priority to hire people who are fundamentally happy and positive.

Even one unhappy, negative person can cause untold damage by focusing on the negative and bringing everyone else down. If you have more than one energy vampire, they create a vampire nest and reinforce each other's feelings of unhappiness and victimhood. You don't want this headache. Besides, your business is not equipped to provide the therapeutic help these folks need.

Our case-study enterprise had an equity partner who didn't fit our criteria for an "A" Player. His perfectionism made the founder's perfectionism look like he wasn't even trying. This manifested itself in his courtship of many demanding and labor-intensive clients who didn't fit the agreed-upon client profile for the business. Ultimately, we decided that the partner's penchant for focusing on the negative ("I must take these bad clients or I won't have any business at all!") was an energy drain to the future success of the business, so he was bought out and replaced.

High-performance habit: Hire happy people who match your core values and are passionate about their role, intelligent, and emotionally intelligent.

How to hire "A" Players

1. **Create a profile of success for the position**. What are the duties of the position? More specifically, what are the knowledge, skills, and abilities (KSAs) required to succeed at a high level? A great place to get this information is by studying employees who are already successful in the job (if this information is available to you).

Do candidates need to have the potential to grow beyond the current position and contribute at a higher level over time? Be clear on the core values of your business that new hires need to embrace in order to succeed.

Prioritize how important these main areas are to success in the job. What percentage of 100% does an area demand? Score candidates against this template for success. For example, sales ability might represent 50% of a success formula for a sales manager position, but would also include leadership and management skills.

Have your interviewers grade candidates on the essential skills for the job. You can then compare tabulated grades among job candidates when the interviews are complete. This process can help in focusing decision-making conversations on actual performance instead of interviewers' Individual biases.

Try a 5-point scale:

- 1 is F, or failing.
- 2 is D, or below average.
- 3 is C, or average.
- 4 is B, or above average.
- 5 is A, or excellent.

2. **Gather pre-interview information**. Past behavior is one of the best predictors of future behavior, and many say it's the very best predictor. Use the resume's biographical information and test for personality, general intellect, management potential, etc., depending on the position in question. In addition, always look for people who are basically happy and positive and who can work well with others.

It is infinitely easier to train technical skills than to change someone's core personality. So, as a general rule of thumb, it's easier to change people than to change people. It's nice to help people, but how much of your resources do you want to dedicate to setting up a rehabilitation clinic within your business?

First of all, unless you're a trained psychologist, you're probably not qualified to do that kind of therapeutic work. Second, everyone is better served leaving it to the professionals who can do this work not only better, but also more cost effectively than you can. Last, always seek advice on how to comply with all employment laws in your area.

3. **Use behavioral interviews**. Interviews are notoriously inconsistent in predicting future job performance. One of the best ways to address this problem is through interviews focused on behavior. For example, you could ask, "Tell me about a time that you got great results by building a strong team," which focuses on the past. Or, you can focus on future behavior by asking, "How would you deal with a high-performing employee whose performance decreased dramatically and quickly?"

When you conduct multiple interviews, have each interviewer focus on one aspect of performance instead of everyone asking the same set of general questions. For example, one interviewer can focus on the ability to build a strong team and another can focus on strategic thinking and planning skills. You'll emerge with a great deal more useable information about the candidate.

You may also want to consider "panel interviews," meaning that several people interview a candidate at the same time. The advantage is that interviewers can later compare observations to triangulate on the important issues to consider. On the other hand, many people have a strong fear of public speaking and a panel turns into an audience of sorts. This can cause otherwise qualified candidates to freeze up, rendered unable to display their skills as well as they might in a less anxiety-producing situation. Consider that factor when deciding if this tool is appropriate for your situation.

It's worth noting that we used all these tools in the case-study firm for this chapter. The results speak for themselves.

High-performance habit: Standardize your hiring process so you can hire "A" Players consistently.

How to be a great coach

Two ways to have teams made up of "A" Players exist:: we can hire them or grow them. Even if we're hiring only A Players and A Player potentials, we still need to know how to coach our employees effectively to the next level of performance. Here are some quick tips for effective coaching:

1. Set clear goals and measures collaboratively with the coachee, with no more than one to three developmental goals at any one time.
2. Grant coachees the autonomy to achieve broad goals their way rather than prescribing the way you'd do it.
3. Make yourself available for regularly scheduled updates, along with real-time learning when needed.
4. Be a cheerleader and motivator, and celebrate successes early and often—your coachees should hear positive feedback at least four times as often as negative feedback.
5. Allay your coachees' unrealistic fears about change—these typically are the obstacles that prevent people from making positive change.
6. Regularly seek feedback from coachees on how you are doing as a

coach.

In individual change and innovation, we must acquire new skills to progress to the next level of performance. As you can see in the figure below, Jim McKinlay's Stairway of Learning (Haines, 2001) posits that we typically progress through several stages of learning.

ACQUIRING NEW SKILLS

LEARNING STAGE	PROCESS	METHOD(S)
UNCONSCIOUS INCOMPETENCE	You don't know what you don't know	Lack of information
CONSCIOUS INCOMPETENCE	You now know what you didn't know	Lecture, discussion
CONSCIOUS COMPETENCE	You can do it with conscious effort	Coaching, practice, feedback
UNCONSCIOUS COMPETENCE	You can do it without conscious effort	Practice, feedback, coaching

In the beginning, we don't know what we don't know. This means that continuously exposing ourselves to new situations and new information will help us discover what skills we need to take our performance to the next level. To reach the skill stage of unconscious competence as quickly as possible, we need training, coaching, and practice. These learning stages help dispel the unrealistic expectation that leaders can send employees to a one-time training class and expect them to effectively acquire new skills.

As part of my agreement with the CEO of the case-study firm for this chapter, I provided individual executive coaching for her and the other members of the senior leadership team. Their individual leadership skills became increasingly stronger over time, and this contributed greatly to the overall success of the firm. One payoff for these efforts is that they all did very well financially when the firm was sold.

High-performance habit: Be a great coach so you can get the very best from your "A" Players.

High-Performance Habits Checklist

☐ Create a business with 90% "A" Players and "A" Player Potentials.

☐ Spend most of your time and money helping your "A" Players make your business more successful rather than "fixing" underperformers.

☐ Hire happy people who match your core values and are passionate about their role, intelligent, and emotionally intelligent.

☐ Standardize your hiring process so you can hire "A" Players consistently.

☐ Be a great coach so you can get the very best from your "A" Players.

☐ Set clear goals and measures collaboratively with the coachee, with no more than one to three developmental goals at any one time.

☐ Limit fear of change and other obstacles that prevent people from making positive change.

☐ Regularly seek feedback from coachees on how you are doing as a coach.

Next, in "Doc"trine #6, we'll explore how to wake up those sleeper employees who are just waiting to excel!

"DOC"TRINE #6: DON'T TURN EAGLES INTO TURKEYS

Let people do what they love and what they're good at.

The Payoff

The members of your team are passionate about what they do, producing at maximum capacity and wildly successful (and now you understand that everybody doesn't have to be good at everything).

"Doc"trine #6 in Action: The Sleeper

It's not that Sally wanted to be contrary; she just felt frustrated and stymied much of the time. She was bright and creative with lots of business savvy, and she was ambitious. A minority-stock partner in a professional services firm, she didn't have the decision-making clout to convince her partners to be more entrepreneurial. Her ideas of reasonable risk and those of her partners were miles apart.

Sally was a great salesperson, however, and she talked her partners into working with me to take the firm to the next level of financial performance. In fact, after our first strategic planning and performance improvement retreat, the entire group rated our efforts a 10 out of 10 when evaluating the meeting.

After some coaching and planning, she quickly emerged from her self-limiting "cocoon" and morphed into a charismatic leader and deal maker. She soon launched a new division of the firm which had considerably more profit potential than the firm's existing business model.

Don't ask a quarterback to play lineman

Being an "A" Player is specific to a job role, so play to each person's passions and talents. If you know anything at all about football, you understand that the skills it takes to be a good quarterback are vastly different from those required to be a good lineman. Yet, I often see leaders put their best players into positions in which they are destined to fail, like Sally in the story above. Don't do that. Sally wasn't a good fit as a lineman, she was a natural quarterback.

True happiness and success have a great deal to do with this fit between people's passions and talents and their environments. Think about some of the most successful people you know. Isn't this true for them?

Consider Phil Jackson, the winningest coach in National Basketball Association history. Clearly, he is passionate about basketball—he won one of his 11 championships as a player in New York. His passion for the game inspired him to develop his skills as a coach and win 10 more championships in that role. I think we'd all agree that Phil has made a lot of money over the years as well.

On the subject of making a lot of money, look at Richard Branson. He was born to be an entrepreneur. He wasn't a huge fan of school, at least partly due to dyslexia, so he ended his formal education after high school. But from a young age he was an entrepreneur and risk taker, trying various money making businesses while still in school. What a loss it would have been for all of us if he had followed the one-size-fits-all advice of "stay in school so you can get a good job."

Now, how about your team? Do you have salespeople who can't sell or production people who can't produce? Before you replace them, consider the possibility that they may be in the wrong role for their passions and talents.

High-performance habit: Remember that being an "A" Player is specific to a job role— the same person could be a "D" Player in a different role.

High-performance habit: Put people in roles in which they can do what they love and what they're good at.

Help people succeed—fire them

Leaders often wrestle with firing employees who aren't performing well. If you care about other people, and all really good leaders do, then it's easy to feel responsible for the welfare of your employees and their families. Stop doing that to yourself!

Caring about someone doesn't mean taking responsibility for their happiness or success. Even if you wanted to take on that job, you don't have the authority or control over this person's life you'd need to do a good job of it. You're assigning yourself responsibility without authority, and we all know that's a formula for needless stress and failure.

If individuals aren't succeeding in their roles and you've already tried role fit assessment and coaching then you can't create a win-win situation. Firing these employees will:

1. Deliver the pain of realizing that they're not succeeding now, which will
2. Give them the opportunity and motivation to find a different situation in which they *can* succeed

You truly are helping these people succeed by taking away the option to continue on the path of failure that they are currently on. What a wonderful and generous leader you are! As strange as it may seem, sometimes firing people is part of doing good.

High-performance habit: If role fit and coaching changes haven't worked, then fire someone so they can truly succeed somewhere else.

High-Performance Habits Checklist

- ☐ Evaluate your Players in their specific job roles—an "A" Player in one role could be a "D" Player in a different job.
- ☐ Put people in roles in which they can do what they love and what they're good at.
- ☐ If role fit and coaching changes haven't worked, then fire those individuals so they can truly succeed somewhere else.

Even if you have everyone in their exact right roles, that doesn't necessarily protect your business from conflict. In "Doc"trine, #7, you'll learn not to fear conflict, but use it as an opportunity to effect valuable positive change.

"DOC"TRINE # 7: WIN WITH WIN-WIN

Resolving inevitable conflicts constructively is essential to building a high-performance business.

The Payoff

Your team resolves inevitable conflicts constructively and efficiently and is much more productive and successful (and who knew that caring about someone means you sometimes want to strangle them?).

"Doc"trine #7 in Action: The Entrepreneurial Couple

A husband-and-wife entrepreneurial team had created a successful architectural design firm. He was the architect and the CEO of the firm, and she was the Vice President of Marketing. In addition, they had two other partners in the firm. The husband contacted me because of a "lack of teamwork in the partner group."

When I assessed their situation, I found a significant amount of unresolved conflict among the partners that had decreased effective teamwork. The husband was a nice, nurturing person, but less assertive than would have been ideal, especially given his role as CEO. For a number of reasons, the two other partners were unhappy that the wife worked in the business, despite the fact that she was good at her job.

After some teambuilding, conflict resolution training, and strategic planning, the wife decided to leave the business. The couple realized their business relationship had overtaken their personal relationship. They were talking about the business constantly and fighting about what should be done with it. In addition, they had to consider the festering resentment coming from the other two partners.

Think about the strain of the situation. When we're at home at dinner after a long day of work, about the last thing we want to hear is: "You know, I really didn't like the way you handled that employee situation today..."

Not only did they have to agree on general life values and priorities and how to raise a family, but now they had to agree on how to run a successful business! They decided that their personal relationship, their first priority, was suffering. They also decided it made more sense for the husband to stay in the business since he had the architectural credentials and experience.

Teamwork in the partner group increased dramatically, and the firm also grew dramatically in revenue and profit. The wife founded her own successful business, and the husband and wife discovered they were much happier in their marriage without work playing such a huge role in their relationship. Both husband and wife found that they were happier, making more money, and doing more good in the marketplace.

Make sure your team reaches the "Performing" stage of development

Bruce Tuckman (1965) observed that groups tend to progress through several stages of development. His Dr. Seuss-like rhyming names for these stages help to make them more memorable (see the figure below).

STAGES OF GROUP DEVELOPMENT

- Forming: being polite
- Storming: resolving inevitable disagreements
- Norming: this is what we do and how we do it
- Performing: achieving your vision

Ambiguity & unresolved conflict kill performance

Forming: Group members are just getting to know one another, so everyone tends to be polite and put their best social foot forward to make a good impression and to preserve the peace.

Storming: Inevitable disagreements and conflicts arise. It's a safe bet that if you put even two people in a room together, they aren't going to agree about everything. When you add more people, you'll have more conflicts. There's no way to avoid conflict altogether, so high performance teams must become adept at resolving it constructively.

Norming: If the group does become adept, it moves to the next stage of development in which people decide on the written (and unwritten) rules that govern the behavior of the group. For example, "It is more important to tell the truth than to protect the ego of the CEO" or "We will conduct all our affairs with integrity." Remember core values? These rules allow the group to avoid unnecessary future conflicts by agreeing on "how we do things around here" beforehand.

Performing: The last stage of development we'll discuss. (The fifth stage is Adjourning; it doesn't rhyme and it's not useful for our purposes.) When the group reaches this stage, it is highly efficient and effective at accomplishing its objectives.

Tuckman maintains that the stages are not intended to be absolutely linear and sequential. A group can be in more than one stage at one time, but they do tend to progress as listed to get to the Performing stage. Clearly this is where we want our teams and our businesses to be!

Using our entrepreneurial couple as a case study for this chapter, conflict between them and among the partners kept the firm stuck in the "Storming" stage of group development. After some planning and conflict resolution training and facilitation, the firm began to actualize its full financial potential.

High-performance habit: For top business performance, make sure your team can resolve inevitable conflicts constructively.

Do you have the right amount of team conflict?

"Groupthink" (Janis, 1972) is a term used to describe a phenomenon whereby a group makes bad decisions because of its strong desire to avoid conflicting opinions within the group. A classic example of groupthink is the Bay of Pigs Invasion of Cuba in 1961. A group of 1,400 paramilitary Cuban expatriates funded by the Central Intelligence Agency (CIA) invaded Cuba from Guatemala with the intent of overthrowing the socialist government of Fidel Castro. The invasion was a complete catastrophe; it lacked any real chance of success, and many people were killed unnecessarily.

The root cause for this disaster was deemed to be a lack of "pushback" or constructive conflict among the people who made the decision to invade in this manner. For a variety of reasons, the people involved felt a need to "go along with the group," even though many had valid concerns about the wisdom of this catastrophically bad decision.

As we can see, it's not desirable to eliminate all conflict in your team. Like George Patton famously said, "If everybody is thinking alike, then somebody isn't thinking." Different perspectives and ideas are healthy— your team just needs to be adept at resolving these conflicts.

OPTIMUM CONFLICT LEVEL FOR MAXIMUM PERFORMANCE

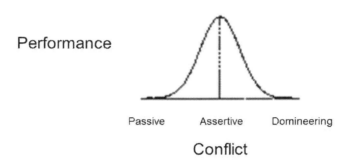

Performance

Passive   Assertive   Domineering

Conflict

As a matter of fact, there IS an "I" in team: TEIM ™

"There's no 'I' in team." I've seen this aphorism on break room bulletin boards more often than I care to remember. It's one of the most destructive popular slogans I've ever heard, and it's the poster child for misinformation and mistrust in businesses.

As a trained psychologist, I know firsthand that it's terrible psychology. I can't imagine telling my clients in good conscience that it is not okay to put themselves and their families first. If they aren't responsible for taking care of themselves and their families, then who is? Remember responsibility and accountability?

What teams really need is independent thinking innovators. They need to understand the value of teamwork for themselves and for the business family. As leaders, you need to encourage independent thinking and constructive disagreement, and then decide what you're going to do to ensure that the whole team wins.

WIIFM truly is the most powerful radio station in the world--(What's In It For Me?). One of the most damaging myths perpetuated on humanity is that you should always put others before yourself. There are times when it makes sense to put others (e.g., your family, your team) before yourself, but these should be the exceptions rather than the rule. For goodness sake, if you're not responsible for taking care of yourself and seeking your own satisfaction and happiness, then who is?

It's worth noting that diverse teams (e.g., age, race, gender, ethnicity, personality, skills) are more productive than less diverse teams because the variety in perspectives results in better decisions. However, this in only true if the team can successfully resolve its conflicts, because a more diverse team will experience more differences of opinion and conflict.

High-performance habit: Make sure there a healthy level of disagreement in your team.

What's your roadmap for resolving conflicts constructively?

My favorite mentor used to say, "If you haven't fantasized about strangling someone with your bare hands, then you don't really care about them." That's an odd point of view, isn't it? But think about it. You don't really care that much about what strangers think about you or about some brief interaction with them. On the other hand, people you depend upon in your team or your business can have a profound effect on your happiness and success. They are important in your life, and you're likely to have strong feelings about them—perhaps strongly liking them when they please you and strongly disliking them when they don't.

The same mentor also used to say, "Be artful with your anger." Anger in itself is healthy and natural, and it can energize you to get what you want. Ignored or used in the wrong way, anger can be destructive. I've seen leaders who think that anger is bad altogether, and they make the mistake of trying to never feel angry. This can result in a "build and burst" pattern of expression in which they store up a great deal of anger before they express it, lose their tempers, and wind up damaging relationships. As with many things, anger management is all about balance between the two extremes of "never angry" and "always angry."

What you do after you get angry makes the real difference in the results you get. The phrase "losing your temper" comes from metallurgy. When a sword is overheated during construction, the metal becomes brittle and breaks easily, just as we become brittle and "break" easily when we allow ourselves to become overheated. To repeat, it's about balance. Your emotions and your reason are designed to work in balance and harmony. Allowing your emotions to overwhelm your reason seldom produces the outcome you want and vice versa. See the figure below for The Conflict/Stress Decision Tree™.

CONFLICT/STRESS DECISION TREE℠

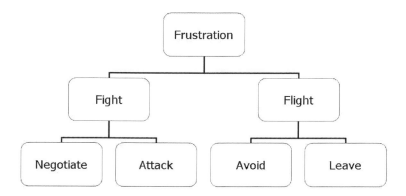

When you're frustrated or angry with a person, you have a choice of fight or flight. If you choose flight, you can avoid the situation or leave the relationship altogether. If you choose fight, then you can attack the other person or take some time to think clearly about what you want out of the situation. The pause-and-think choice maximizes your chances of negotiating the outcome you want.

I coached a leader who was very bright and hard charging. So much so, in fact, that she was apt to be impatient and lose her temper with people when frustrated. We worked on her "ready, fire, aim" approach to handling her anger and improved it markedly. She trained herself to slow down and consider her options when she was angry so that she didn't do unnecessary damage to her business and personal relationships.

The figure below is the Thomas-Kilmann model (1974) of conflict management, the most popular conflict management model in the world.

CONFLICT MANAGEMENT STYLES

As you can see, the vertical axis is concern for yourself, or assertiveness, and the horizontal axis is concern for others, or consideration (also cooperation or teamwork). The model posits that we all use all the conflict management styles at different times and in different situations (e.g., you may be assertive at home but less so at work), but that we tend to have a primary go-to style that we use most often.

When we can make it happen, the Collaborate, or win-win style in the top right quadrant, is ideal. We are both assertive and considerate, and each party feels good about the outcome. This style is particularly effective for conflicts that occur inside your business among its employees.

The top left quadrant is Compete/Force or win-lose style. In this style you are assertive but not considerate, so you essentially bully the other party. Sometimes this style is unavoidable, as when the other party isn't willing to negotiate or when a supervisor must make a decision that is best for the group but may be harmful to an individual. In addition, this win-lose style works in the U.S. economy. In our system, you don't get much payoff in being extra considerate to competitors vying for the same dollars your business is also going after.

The bottom right quadrant is the Accommodate or lose-win style. In this style you are considerate but not assertive. You essentially take a "doormat" or "martyr" position in the conflict by sacrificing what is in your best interests so that the others can get what they want. A positive use of this style happens when you temporarily take a pay cut during an economic downturn so the rest of your team gets paid, and you stay in the business for the long term.

The bottom left quadrant is the Avoid or lose-lose style. In this style neither party gets what it wants. Essentially, you act like an ostrich with your head in the sand. However, there might be times that a conflict is a one-time fleeting event that isn't worth investing time and energy into. In that situation this style may be the best choice. For example, if you know someone is saying negative and inaccurate things about you at work, one viable strategy is to ignore it. Here, the assumption is that gossip eventually hurts the person spreading it, and that happens as a natural outcome and you don't need to do anything.

Compromise is essentially the fifth style, and it's directly in the middle of the graph. In this style, both parties get some of what they want, but neither feels really good about it. Generally, the better strategy is to continue to negotiate (if possible) until a collaborative win-win solution can be achieved. Still, sometimes compromise may be the best choice.

Finally, the sixth option is to call "No Deal" and walk away from the negotiation or the relationship. For example, if a job seeker and a potential employer cannot come to mutually agreeable terms, they're better off not compromising and moving on to a potential win-win relationship.

You can rate your own primary (and secondary) style using this model, but most people put themselves in the Collaborate (win-win) quadrant. If we thought we weren't in this quadrant, we'd likely be doing something differently. It's much more revealing and useful, however, to ask other members of your team to place you in a quadrant. If you take this approach, I strongly recommend you use a trained facilitator—it can be a powerfully positive experience if done well and a powerfully negative experience if done poorly.

Going back to our husband-wife case study, in order to reach the result we ended up with, it was necessary to create a win-win-win scenario in which all the stakeholders in the situation got something they felt good about. For example, when the wife decided to leave the business, she was pleased her husband and partner supported her use of some of their financial resources to launch a new business that she was passionate about.

High-performance habit: When possible, shoot for a Win-Win resolution to conflicts by caring about yourself AND the other person.

"You catch more flies with honey…"

You have two basic ways to change your own or someone else's behavior. This is particularly important to leaders because the biggest part of their role isn't to get as much work done as they can, but rather, to inspire others to get as much work done as they can.

1.   **Pain.** You definitely can change someone's behavior if you have the power and control to punish them and cause them pain. Coercion works very well in some situations—you can hold a gun to someone's head and he or she most likely will do whatever you say as long as you keep the gun there. In a less-than-free social systems, such as a prison, those with the power and control (the guards) can coerce the prisoners to do things.

Guilt is another powerful form of punishment. If you can convince people that whatever they are doing is bad in some way, then they'll be open to direction about what they can do to be "good" again. For example, if you want people to work longer hours, you can call them "lazy" if they say they want to spend time with their family and friends. If they believe they're actually lazy, then they'll work longer hours to win your approval and not be called lazy any more.

This coercion technique also can work well at the group level, in which case we call it peer pressure. We humans are pack animals, and to be truly happy we need approval and support from others. This is biologically programmed behavior that helps ensure our survival as a species. Some leaders manipulate this human need when they want to change someone else's behavior.

But there are three main problems with the pain-and-punishment method of changing behavior:

a. **It's temporary.** You have to keep that gun to people's heads, or you have to keep inviting them to feel guilty about what they're doing. Left to their own devices, folks likely will go back to doing what they were doing before.

b. **It's labor intensive.** This approach requires a lot of ongoing effort. Chasing someone around trying to make them do things they don't really want to do is hard work. If you are from "the beatings will continue until morale improves" school of leadership, just think of all the time and energy you will have to expend administering those beatings.

c. **People dislike you.** People almost always resent being punished. Consider, too, that those who enjoy being punished may not be the most emotionally well-adjusted folks to be employees in your business. While being liked isn't always possible, in general it makes your job as a leader much easier if you enjoy someone's goodwill.

2. **Pleasure.** You can change people's behavior with a pleasurable reward they value. Too often leaders think money is the only important motivator for work behavior. It's not. Of course, it's important to pay fair market-rate compensation if you want to attract and retain good people, but after that, things such as recognition, autonomy, and growth opportunities motivate people more than additional money. If you double people's salary, you aren't likely to get double production from them.

Healthy people are motivated by enlightened self-interest. For example, being a member of a team can be frustrating and inconvenient in the short term (e.g., meetings, miscommunication, conflict), but you know that you can win bigger individually by being part of a high-performance team. Therefore, a bit of enlightened patience in the beginning can result in a bigger individual payoff in the end.

There are three main reasons that reward works well to change behavior:

a. **It can be long lasting.** You can put a reward system in place (e.g., a bonus program) that will continue to motivate positive work behavior.

b. **It's not labor intensive.** You don't have to be "chasing someone with a stick" to get them to do what you want. People are internally motivated to seek the reward without you having to provide external effort. Also, their internal motivation tends to be self-perpetuating.

c. **People like you.** Once again, being liked as a leader is not always achievable, but having the goodwill of those in your business has many benefits, especially when you want them to help you achieve the goals of your business. They are more likely to "go the extra mile" for you if they believe you have already done that for them.

Candidly, you need both pain and pleasure in your tool belt to motivate others. Like a good parent, if you use only pleasure, you will wind up with a spoiled follower who has no respect for boundaries or other people. Folks need to know that the team's best interests and agreements will be enforced. However, you should use pleasure as a motivator at least four times as often as pain, because painful memories are much stronger than pleasurable ones. You don't want people cringing or running for the hills when they see you coming.

High-performance habit: In trying to change the behavior of others, most of the time you'll get better results using pleasure as a motivator rather than pain.

How to get what you want in a conflict situation

When dealing with conflict, you'll get better results keeping things FABulous ™. That is, focus on Feelings And Behavior. Talk about your feelings and the other person's behavior. For example you might say, "I feel frustrated when you talk so much and don't give me a chance to talk, too." But you get into trouble if instead you said, "You don't care about me because you never listen to me." You're talking about the other person's feelings. Unless you're some kind of psychic, you can't truly know how someone else is feeling.

When we attribute the wrong feelings to someone else, they usually get angry with us because they feel unjustly accused. Clearly this isn't a good thing when you're trying to resolve a conflict.

To go a step further, when in a conflict with another person, employ the BARB ™ system of feedback:

- **Behavior:** talk about it, rather than character or feelings
- **Affects you:** how?
- **Request:** alternative behavior
- **Benefits:** of doing things differently

For example, instead of saying, "You're sneaky and dishonest," you could say, "When you pad your expense account, I worry that you may be distorting facts elsewhere and that I may not be able to trust you. If you were more accurate with your expense account, you'd begin to earn my trust back, which means I wouldn't have to fire you for a lack of integrity."

As we've seen, if you're in the middle of a conflict, one of the last things you want to do is lose your temper. At that point, you can't think clearly and are likely to do something you'll regret later. A technique useful in this situation is "reflecting." Before you respond, you summarize what the other person has said.

For example, if someone were to say, "You're ugly, and your mother dresses you funny," you might get angry. But instead of attacking the person in return, you could say, "I'm a little surprised by what you said. Let me see if I heard you correctly. You said that you think I'm unattractive, that my mother picks out my clothes, and that she has poor taste in clothes. Is that right?"

There are at least three advantages to this technique: It:

1. Gives you time to pause and think before you respond.
2. Gives the person an opportunity to clarify what she really meant in case you misunderstood her.
3. Allows you time to think rationally and dissect the message logically, which can sound much less inflammatory when examined more closely. When you reflect on the example above, it sounds improbable, mean-spirited, and just plain silly, rather than hurtful.

You can be sure that we employed all the techniques above in engineering the results we achieved with our husband-wife case study firm. There were some tense moments that were diffused by these techniques and some good, cool-headed thinking.

High-performance habit: To get what you want from others, talk about your feelings, their behavior, and what's in it for them to do what you want.

Think of sales as a special case of conflict resolution

I've learned more sales techniques than Zig Ziglar has closed deals, and I see the sales dance as a special case of conflict resolution as the salesperson and the prospect try to get to a win-win relationship (as in all business relationships). Here's my take on sales:

1. **Get back to basics.** Drop the gimmicks. People want to buy what they need from someone who a) is competent and b) cares about their happiness. If you're not both of these, then you don't deserve the sale. The first sale is always to yourself. Would you buy from you?

2. **Be authentic.** Stop trying to BS your way into a sale. Being honest with prospects. Who wants to do business with someone he can't trust? If you're not the best choice for your prospect, say so. If you think your prospect is making a mistake or missing an opportunity, say so. The good karma will come back to you in the long run.

3. **Listen a lot more than you talk.** Stop selling and start listening. As they say, you've got two ears and one mouth—use that as a guide. How can you truly help others if you don't listen long enough to find out what they really need? Ask lots of questions. Sometimes prospects don't really know what they need, and you can help them figure that out.

High-performance habit: Think of sales as special case of conflict resolution in which you're trying to get to a Win-Win solution.

High-Performance Habits Checklist

- ☐ For top business performance, make sure your team can resolve inevitable conflicts constructively.
- ☐ Make sure there's a healthy level of disagreement in your team.
- ☐ When possible shoot for a Win-Win resolution by caring about yourself AND the other person.
- ☐ In trying to change the behavior of others, most of the time you'll get better results using pleasure as a motivator rather than pain.
- ☐ To get what you want from others, talk about your feelings, their behavior, and what's in it for them to do what you want.
- ☐ Think of sales as special case of conflict resolution in which you're trying to get to a Win-Win solution.

We live in the age of data, and the data-driven business is typical today. That's why "Doc"trine #8 is all about measuring—and doing it with a purpose—a few of them, actually.

"DOC"TRINE #8: MEASURE SUCCESS

It's a lot more fun and profitable to go somewhere than to go nowhere.

The Payoff

Your followers are excited about achieving clear, measurable goals for themselves and the business (and everyone is shocked that all this isn't mind-numbingly complex).

"Doc"trine #8 in Action: The Data-Driven Business

A family business experienced declining revenues and poor morale among its employees, and the patriarch and CEO was completely stymied about why this was occurring. He didn't know which way to turn, and the stress was damaging his relationships with other family members who worked in the business. He was extremely frustrated and discouraged about the business he'd worked so hard to build.

We had the Leadership Team rate the performance of the business with the Leading Indicator Evaluation ™, and the results were eye-opening. Using a numerical scale that translated into a grading system of measurement (5 = excellent = A, 4 = above average = B, 3 = average = C, 2 = below average = D, 1 = failing = F), we discovered that the leadership team thought that the business was below average on several important factors.

Business goals and roles were unclear. While it would be an exaggeration to say that everybody felt responsible for everything, it was true that most of the leaders weren't clear on exactly what they were responsible for. In addition, we saw a pervasive concern about the negative effects of nepotism on business performance. Family members were seen as receiving favored treatment and opportunities, which weren't based on performance. This was perceived as unfair and demotivating for non-family members.

We created a comprehensive program of individual and team performance improvement that included significant changes to the organizational structure and roles, as well as individual coaching for all members of the leadership team. In addition, non-family leaders were provided more opportunity and clearer paths to achieve their individual goals. Within a few months morale and motivation had improved significantly and the business was growing rapidly.

Measure what you want to get done

We've all seen how what gets measured gets done, haven't we? The mere act of setting a goal and measuring progress makes us pay more attention to achieving it and less attention to other things. How will you know if you've arrived at your destination if you don't choose one? Building a "data driven" business has many advantages, the primary one being that both major and minor decisions are easier if you have the right information to base them on.

I'd like measurement to be one of your new best friends. I recommend that you institutionalize the three-stage measurement cycle into your business:

1. Measure
2. Improve
3. Repeat forever

Doing this ensures that you're clear about what's important to your business success and you'll know whether you're succeeding. You'll find it much less likely that your efforts are diluted by "shiny object" distractions that are "nice to do" but aren't really important to your success.

While it's valuable to be aware of inputs, or "leading indicators" (e.g., sales calls), it's even more valuable to be aware of outputs, or "lagging indicators" (e.g., sales revenue). Otherwise, you can get caught up in "working hard" versus "working smart." Do you really want to track how much time your salespeople spend in the office, or are you more interested in how many sales and satisfied return customers they generate? Sales mean happiness and making money, but frenzied, unfocused efforts, no matter how much they look like hard work rarely lead to a sense of wellbeing.

High-performance habit: Measure the things regularly that are important to your success.

Use this simple measure to get a bird's-eye view of your business

When I'm first talking with leaders about their businesses, I have them plug in two numbers to the Financial Performance Prediction Model ™ below. This tells us a lot about where their business financial performance is now, and what changes we need to make to improve that performance.

The model divides business financial performance into individual performance and team performance. The mythical ideal high-performance business would have 100% individual performance and 100% team performance. I say mythical because this kind of perfection is an unattainable ideal rather than a realistic goal for business leaders. It still holds true, however, that the closer we get to 100% in these two areas, the better our financial performance will be.

100% individual performance includes:

1.   All "A" Players or "A" Player Potentials
2.   All Players coached to their full potential
3.   All Players happy and motivated

100% team performance includes:

1.   A great strategic plan
2.   Great implementation of that plan
3.   A great continuous innovation system

Would a business like this be great, or what? In the model, the relationship between individual and team performance is multiplicative rather than additive because these two components of the model interact with each other in a more complex way than a purely additive relationship. For example, if you have strong individual performance in your business but weak team performance, the weak team performance will decrease the impact of your strong individual performers.

If you have a $1,000,000 business, and you have 80% individual performance (e.g., generally strong followers) and 60% team performance (e.g., less than strong implementation of your strategy) you would be getting 48% of the potential financial performance of your business. If you were to increase individual performance to 90% (e.g., improve your training and coaching program) and team performance to 90% (e.g., improve implementation of your strategy), you would achieve 81% of the financial performance potential of the business, a net increase of 33%, or about $333,000.

The idea here is that if you improve either individual performance or team performance, then financial performance always improves. Imagine the kind of improvement in financial performance you'll get if you improve both at the same time! Now that's being happier, making more money, and doing more good in the world!

A quick caveat:: Before my academic colleagues feast on the lack of mathematical precision of this model, let me say that the model is not meant to be an exact mathematical formula. It is intended to inform and inspire leaders about what changes they can make to improve the financial performance of their businesses. The model passes the most important test of any model—it works.

High-performance habit: To maximize financial performance, work toward 100% individual performance and 100% team performance.

Be a SKEPTIC about changes in your external environment

Think of strategic planning as a group of people on a moving train having a meeting about where they want to go. The whole time the group is deciding on a destination, the scenery and their location are constantly changing. This is one reason I favor Steve Haines' SKEPTIC tool (2007) for scanning the external environment for current and future trends to be aware of during strategic planning. Keep in mind that you're creating a plan based on assumptions about the trends in the world outside your business that may affect your success in the next three to five years and beyond.

It's wise to monitor these regularly because the world is changing rapidly. I recommend tracking at least the top three trends in each category of the model and updating your environmental scan quarterly. The SKEPTIC model categories are:

- **Socio-demographic**
  - o Example: "Boomers will be leaving the workforce en masse, leaving big gaps in leadership skills and institutional knowledge."
- **Competition/substitutes** (the British spelling of skeptic is "sceptic")
  - o Example: "Due to the low barriers to entry into our industry, we will have more but smaller competitors."
- **Economics**
  - o Example: "The U.S. economy will continue to recover steadily, with no major correction in the next five years."
- **Ecology/environment** (yes, we're now actually at a "sceeptic" acronym, but you get the idea)
  - o Example: "Green building will become even more important."
- **Political/Regulatory**
  - o Example: "Federal corporate taxes will be lowered to be more in line with international standards."
- **Technology**
  - o Example: "Mobile phones will continue to become the portal of choice for accessing information."
- **Industry/Suppliers**
  - o Example: "Our industry will continue to consolidate into a few big players."
- **Customers**
  - o Example: "Our customers will continue to become more racially and ethnically diverse."

Scan your external environment for trends that can affect the success of your business every three to four months.

High-performance habit: Scan your external environment regularly for trends that can affect the success of your business.

SWOT those pesky ambiguities away

As I've said before, the SWOT Analysis (Strengths, Weaknesses, Opportunities, and Threats; Humphrey, 2005) is a useful strategic planning tool. When evaluating the current state of your business, list the top three to five internal strengths and weaknesses and external opportunities and threats. Here are some examples:

- **Internal strengths**: How do we build on these? Examples: strong senior leadership team, great facility.
- **Internal weaknesses**: How do we eliminate these? Examples: insufficient teamwork, overhead too high.
- **External opportunities**: How do we exploit these? Examples: potential acquisition, entering a new market.
- **External threats**: How do we lessen these? Examples: new government regulations, new competitor.

Some experts recommend using a more detailed form of the SWOT analysis (e.g., using the Malcolm Baldridge National Quality Award criteria as a basis for analysis), but I recommend limiting the focus to three to five items in each category. Otherwise, the analysis can be too broad and we lose focus by attempting to attend to too many variables at one time. I recommend conducting a SWOT analysis every three to four months.

Don't LIE ™ to yourself about the effectiveness of your processes

I consider myself a process consultant. If you get the right processes in place (e.g., hire the right people, create a great strategic plan, etc.), you'll get great business results. In the figure below you'll see I've created a measure for that purpose based on the 12 principles presented as the chapter titles of this book (see below).

LEADING INDICATOR EVALUATION ™

Please rate your leadership team from 1 to 5 on how it is currently performing.

1 = Failing = F
2 = Below Average = D
3 = Average = C
4 = Above Average = B
5 = Excellent = A

LEADING INDICATOR	"A" STANDARD	Rating
Harness happiness	Members are happy & motivated	
Be someone worth following	Our leaders are great examples	
Field a pro team	Members are top 10% performers in their roles, or can be soon	
Don't turn eagles into turkeys	Members' roles fit their talents well	
Win with win-win	Conflicts are resolved effectively	
Focus your vision	Goals are clear, focused, & prioritized	
Value your values	Core values are followed consistently	
Measure success	We are measuring the right things	
Delegate	Authority is delegated effectively	
Clarify roles & accountability	Roles & accountabilities are clear, follow through is consistent	
Create teamwork	High level of teamwork & synergy	
Institutionalize innovation	High level of continuous innovation	
TOTAL		
OVERALL AVERAGE SCORE (Total divided by 12)		
OVERALL PERFORMANCE "GRADE" 1 = F, 2 = D, 3 = C, 4 = B 4.5 = A		

In my work, I'm usually giving the LIE ™ to the senior leadership team of a business, but it can be used with any team at any level in the company. I typically administer this survey at the same time as the SWOT Analysis to identify causes for celebration and opportunities for to improve performance. All individual responses are kept confidential, and I report only the average of the team's ratings. This encourages a higher level of honest feedback from those completing the ratings. Lastly, I like using a 1-5 scale tied to grades of A-F since most people are familiar with this grading system.

High-performance habit: Conduct a focused SWOT Analysis and a LIE ™ every three to four months to monitor the important strengths and opportunities for improvement in your business.

Track the Core Success Measures

I favor tracking the following six core measures of success in order to achieve business success (Haines, 2007):

1. **Financial performance**. Examples: revenue, profit.
2. **Customer satisfaction**. Examples: overall satisfaction rating, willingness to recommend your business to others.
3. **Employee satisfaction**. Examples: overall satisfaction rating, willingness to recommend your business to others.
4. **Operational efficiency**. Examples: inventory turns, profit per employee.
5. **Performance versus competitors**. Examples: market share, performance vs. an industry benchmark.
6. **Contribution to society**. Examples: number of homes built to house families, number of businesses helped become more profitable.

Financial performance is obvious (e.g., profit): we don't get to stay if we don't pay our bills.

Customer satisfaction is also obvious: Satisfied customers are the financial lifeblood of our businesses. I've never seen a company with unhappy employees and happy customers, so we need to pay attention to employee and customer satisfaction through regular formal and informal engagement surveys and feedback.

Operational efficiency (e.g., time to order fulfillment) means we're using our resources to the best advantage. Our performance versus that of our competitors (e.g., market share) affects our strategy; we're likely to do things differently depending on whether we have the biggest market share or the smallest.

Finally, making a measurable contribution to society is important because a business needs reasons other than profit to keep its members engaged and fulfilled over time. Remember that making a positive difference in the lives of others is one of the five primary sources of happiness discussed in Chapter One. Harness this drive for happiness to create extraordinary business success.

Create a simple and manageable dashboard

In our world of infinite data available at our fingertips 24/7, leaders are drowning in knowledge and yet thirsty for wisdom. To achieve this focus, you need to create a dashboard of measures that begins with the six basic measures and includes three to five strategic priority goals for your planning horizon (usually 3 to 5 years).

1. Financial performance
2. Customer satisfaction
3. Employee satisfaction
4. Operational efficiency
5. Performance versus competitors
6. Contribution to society
7. Strategic priority #1
8. Strategic priority #2
9. Strategic priority #3
10. Strategic priority #4

I recommend that you have no more than 10 measures overall on your high-level dashboard, which monitors the progress of the strategic plan. You can have more detailed measures in other places, but you don't want to get into the "glacial progress on a thousand different fronts" syndrome; it's overwhelming and demotivating. If you do all these things well, you will have a superlative business that is the envy of all. Now you have nine or ten simple measures you can post on a single page to guide your leadership team in achieving the strategic plan for your business.

While you will have more in-depth measures throughout your business, the dashboard gives you a tool for monitoring progress at the big-picture strategic level that is easy to understand and doesn't overwhelm. Too many leaders get lost in the day-to-day minutia and lose sight of the overall goal.

High-performance habit: Create a focused dashboard that includes the core success measures plus your three to five strategic priorities, and update it monthly.

Create your Strategic Priorities Implementation Plan

When you have your vision and strategic priorities in place, create your implementation plan to focus your time and money on the actions most important to achieving your strategic priorities in the current year. If possible, focus your priority actions to the top three under each strategic priority.

STRATEGIC PRIORITIES IMPLEMENTATION PLAN

Strategic Priority/12-Month Priority Actions	Champ	Due	Person Years Projected	Person Years Actual	Cost Projected	Cost Actual	Yr. 1 goal	Yr. 2 goal	Yr. 3 goal	Current date & measure	Status
Strategic Priority #1: Double our revenue	Fred	June 30, '16	xxx	Xxx	xxx	xxx	xxx	xxx	3M	xxx	Green
1a) Increase production capacity	Sally	July 31, '13	xxx	Xxx	xxx	xxx	xxx			xxx	Yellow
1b) Add staff	Bob	xxx	xxx	Xxx	Xxx	xxx	xxx			xxx	Red
1c) Increase sales	Pam	xxx	xxx	Xxx	Xxx	Xxx	xxx			xxx	Green

High-performance habit: Create an implementation plan which includes three or fewer priority actions for the coming year for each strategic priority.

Align individual goals and business goals

Aligning individual employee goals with overall business goals is incredibly powerful! Imagine the productivity and success you can generate with this alignment in place. So how do we accomplish this? In "Doc"trine #9 I lay out an effective and efficient individual performance management system to help you align individual and business goals.

High-performance habit: Implement an individual performance management system that aligns overall business goals with individual goals and professional development (See Chapter 9).

See all with 360 degree feedback

The idea of 360 degree feedback consists of getting anonymous aggregated feedback from your supervisor, your peers, and your subordinates. As a management tool, 360 degree feedback has its advocates and its critics, but I've found it useful in measuring individual and team performance.

I use this tool only when I'm convinced the leader who holds the power is committed to treating people fairly. I've found the greatest challenge in raising the performance of any team is creating an environment in which people feel comfortable being honest with each other, and especially being honest with their leaders. This is usually impeded by fears of punishment, and these fears are difficult to overcome.

When people are treated fairly in a business, though, conducting a 360 degree feedback exercise can give people an opportunity to be honest anonymously without fear of punishment. This is a way to "unstick" all the energy trapped in fear and use it to restructure the environment to be more supportive of honest communication. And, as covered earlier, without honest communication, we don't have accurate information to successfully run our businesses.

Under normal circumstances, I recommend conducting this analysis only once a year because of the time it requires. It's important to be as efficient as possible with administrative time so that productivity doesn't suffer, and the troops don't rebel and do the exercise half-heartedly.

We can expect differing perspectives on how to use this analysis. Some say it should be used as part of a performance management process. Others think it should be employed only as an individual developmental tool, kept confidential and not shared with the individual's supervisor. I subscribe to the former view. If the business environment is so hostile that this process is considered negative, then that's a sign that other issues need to be addressed first before we use this tool.

One downside of 360 degree feedback is that it can make people feel a little paranoid about who gave them some particular piece of feedback, especially negative feedback: "Was it someone who's opinion I value, or was it that crackpot over in accounting?"

My general advice about negative feedback, and anonymous negative feedback in particular, is before you seriously consider it, look for a repeated pattern of responses rather than an isolated instance. If you do take it under advisement, find a way to get clarification by talking with your raters as a group or individually. After that, consider doing something differently only if there is a clear advantage in doing so. Otherwise, you can fall prey to the "trying to please all the people all the time" syndrome, which we all know is impossible.

Lastly, you can aggregate the 360 degree feedback data into a team profile, which is another useful feature of this tool. In this way you can see the overall areas of strength and weakness in your team. This is a handy way to decide where to focus your training and professional development resources to improve the overall skills of your team.

When I first met the CEO in our case-study business discussed in this chapter, he was shockingly unaware of the roles, goals, and morale problems that his leadership team experienced, and it was hurting the performance of his operation. While he was adept at measuring in-depth business analytics of all sorts, he wasn't measuring the things that made the real difference in his business. When we corrected this problem, he experienced rapid growth and financial success.

High-performance habit: Use 360 degree feedback as a measure of individual (and team) performance one or two times a year.

High-Performance Habits Checklist

- ☐ Measure the things regularly that are important to your success.
- ☐ To maximize financial performance, work toward 100% individual performance and 100% team performance.
- ☐ Scan your external environment for trends that can affect the success of your business every three to four months.
- ☐ Conduct a focused SWOT Analysis and a LIE TM every three to four months to monitor the important strengths and opportunities for improvement in your business.
- ☐ Create a focused dashboard that includes the core success measures plus your three to five strategic priorities and update it monthly.
- ☐ Implement an individual performance management system that aligns overall business goals with individual goals and professional development (See Chapter 9).
- ☐ Use 360 degree feedback as a measure of individual (and team) performance one to two times a year.

Everybody wants to get things done, but oftentimes people aren't completely clear on who's responsible for what. In "Doc"trine #9 we'll look at the best ways to guarantee results through clear roles and accountability.

"DOC"TRINE #9: CLARIFY ROLES AND ACCOUNTABILITY

Teams can't be held accountable—only individuals.

The Payoff

Everyone in your business knows their role and accountability in achieving the vision (and you won't have "I've got it—I thought you had it!" frustration).

"Doc"trine #9 in Action: Who's Got the Ball?

Stage one: A father had founded a family business two decades before and later brought in his two sons to help him run the firm. By the time I met the three of them, the dad had told the sons he wanted to begin stepping away from the business and handing off control to them. However, no one seemed happy with the way that plan was progressing.

First, we clarified the individual future visions of the father and the sons, knowing they could make progress only if they could each meet their individual goals. Then we clarified their roles and accountability within the business. The younger son was naturally analytical and even-tempered, so he was a good fit for the role of company President. The older son was more passionate and a better relationship and business developer, traits that made him a good fit for Vice President of Sales and Marketing.

This was a close knit family, without jealousies or insecurities complicating things—a strong asset. They were also practical in their perspective. The dad was sincere in his wish to relinquish day-to-day control of the business, and the older son was happy with his younger brother occupying the role of President (as long as he got his share of the profits).

Stage two: As with many growing businesses, the key employees of the firm wore several hats and had a wide variety of responsibilities. Employees essentially were viewed as individual profit centers. Overall, they were responsible for their own marketing, sales, and delivery to their clients. Key employees might work across several lines of the business in fulfilling their responsibilities.

The firm didn't achieve economies of scale in shared functions such as marketing. This made it difficult to have clear responsibility and accountability that allowed evaluation of individual performance. If everybody essentially was responsible for everything, how could we tell if any one person was succeeding or not?

We realized that the firm had reached the size that we needed greater role specialization, so we reassigned key employee roles along product lines. These profit centers were much easier to understand and measure, and after some initial resistance to the change, the key employees embraced this approach as a simpler organizational design; it allowed them to distinguish themselves and to achieve their individual goals.

Stage three: We reconfigured and streamlined the Senior Leadership Team to reflect the new emphasis on clear roles and individual accountability. This made the team more nimble, more homogenous in terms of degree of responsibility, and generally more efficient and effective overall. Everyone knew who got credit for what and who to turn to if a problem needed to be fixed. Consequently, and the firm's revenues grew rapidly.

Don't try to hold a team accountable

As with many things in business, ambiguity is the real enemy. When everyone is accountable for *everything*, then no one is really accountable for *anything*. That's why you can't hold teams accountable; only individuals. Clarifying roles and accountability puts an end to the, "I've got it; I thought you had it!" syndrome.

This might sound like a no brainer, but you'd be surprised by how many business leaders leave this area fuzzy and confusing for their teams. That's why it was so important for this family, our case study for this chapter, to first clarify who was going to be accountable for the performance of the firm, the father or one of the sons. In this case, the family made the younger son the President, and he accepted the overall responsibility for the performance of the family business.

Furthermore, if you hold an individual accountable for a goal or role without the matching position authority to get the job done, that won't work either. In our case study, had the older son been unwilling to support his brother in his role as President, the younger brother would have become chronically frustrated by having accountability without authority. That situation would have hurt the overall performance of the business.

I've seen many leaders try to hold teams accountable through "group punishments" for the bad behavior of an individual. For example, imagine a basketball coach making the whole team run wind sprints because one member of the team made a mistake executing a play in practice. These kinds of techniques are intended to foster an "all for one, one for all" culture which some believe lead to higher team performance.

My experience, however, tells me it's a mistake to use this technique. Doing so means leaders abrogate responsibility, essentially delegating their leadership responsibility and authority to their teams. In addition, this approach leads to frustration, conflict, and infighting among team members, because it violates basic fairness. It's important to treat people fairly if you want their best effort. It certainly isn't fair to hold someone accountable for a teammate's performance without the managerial position authority to do so legitimately.

I once worked with a business in which all incentive pay was tied to a team goal. Therefore, regardless of how well individual members of the team performed, they couldn't increase their compensation unless the team goals were met. This compensation system led to hard feelings among the team members when the team didn't meet the goals, and some of the highest performers ended up going elsewhere.

Without role clarity, your conscientious followers will start to become overwhelmed and discouraged. They care deeply about the business doing well, but they don't have clear goals and accountability so they can feel successful and like they're "winning." Since they tend to feel responsible for the success of the entire business, they then think they're chronically falling short in their performance. Over time they'll begin to withdraw their best efforts from your business so they can rebalance their emotions and no longer feel like they're "losing."

There's a really big difference between caring about the performance of the whole business and feeling responsible for the performance of the whole business. Feeling responsible is the role of the leader of the business, and you can't delegate it. If you'd prefer not to have this responsibility, then change your role to "entrepreneur" and hire a CEO to run the company.

High-performance habit: Make sure all your followers know their roles and what they're accountable for.

High-performance habit: Don't hold your followers accountable for the performance of their teammates unless they have the managerial position authority to do so.

Design your organizational structure to fit your needs

In designing the organizational structure of your business, you have three basic choices:

1. **By division.** You also have three basic choices within the division structure:
   a. **By product**. If you make Widgets, Thingamajigs, and Whatchamacallits, you can organize your business around those product lines. You can have a Widget division, a Thingamajig division, and a Whatchamacallit division focused on the success of those products. For example, historically, General Motors has organized itself around car brands like Chevrolet, Buick, and Cadillac.
   b. **By customer**. If you're in the wealth management business and you have clients that have 1M invested and you have clients that have 50M invested, then you might want to organize by customer. You may sell some of the same products to both these clients, but there likely would be some different products and two very different levels of service.
   c. **By geography**. If you have offices in New York and Los Angeles, it might make sense to organize by location because of the challenges of communicating over distances.

You can see the main advantage of the division structure in the clear profit centers and accountability for the success of your products. The main disadvantages typically involve the increase in overhead costs of duplicate support functions such as marketing, human resources, etc. In addition, it can be difficult to create and leverage teamwork synergies among the separate divisions.

2. **By function.** As businesses get larger and more complex, they often adopt a functional structure. They organize themselves by functions such as manufacturing, marketing, human resources, sales, etc. The main advantage to this structure is creating and leveraging teamwork synergies across product lines. The main disadvantage is losing focus on ultimate profitability by shifting focus to internal functions and efficiency.

3. **The matrix.** The matrix organizational structure was created to capitalize on the advantages and address the disadvantages of the division and function organizational designs. In this structure an employee may have reporting relationships with both a product line supervisor and a functional department supervisor. The National Aeronautics and Space Administration (NASA) is the most famous example of this type of structure. The main advantage of this type of design is that it creates and leverages teamwork synergies within the business. The main disadvantage is that it creates a great deal of complexity in communication and coordination (i.e., bureaucracy), and can dilute accountability for profitability. I'm not a huge fan of this structure because it goes against the "KISS" (simpler works better) principle, but for some rare situations it may be the best choice.

High-performance habit: Design your organizational structure to fit your business needs and goals.

Create focused job descriptions

We have a saying in my field of Industrial/Organizational Psychology: "Everything begins with a job description." While this may be a bit of an overstatement, a clear, concise job description is unquestionably the foundation of individual performance. How can you hold people accountable for their performance if their area of responsibility isn't clear? Create a job description for every job in your business.

Answer the question, "What is this person's role in the business?", either for someone doing the job or for someone looking for a job (you certainly want job seekers to be clear on what they're signing up for). The fundamental job description consists of knowledge, skills, and abilities (KSA's) the person needs to succeed in the job. You can include other items, depending upon the level and complexity of the job. (See the sample below).

Remember to keep your job descriptions current. As your business grows in size and complexity, job roles tend to become more specialized and much less "jack of all trades."

Sample Job Description

NAME OF COMPANY:	ABC Company
JOB TITLE:	President
REPORTS TO:	Board Chair
POSITION TYPE:	Full time
TERMS OF EMPLOYMENT:	Ongoing
TRAVEL REQUIREMENTS:	Approximately 25%
LOCATION:	Atlanta, GA
SALARY RANGE:	100-150k
BENEFITS:	Medical, vacation, ongoing training, etc.

POSITION DESCRIPTION (One sentence)

Creates and maintains satisfactory financial performance of the company

CORE VALUES/CULTURAL FIT

- Honest
- Team oriented
- Service oriented

KEY AREAS OF RESPONSIBILITY

- Creates and maintains satisfactory financial performance of the company
- Manages ongoing strategic planning and implementation activities
- Manages all functional department heads

KNOWLEDGE, SKILLS, AND ABILITIES

- Ability to lead and inspire others
- Superior oral and written communication skills

EDUCATION AND EXPERIENCE

- Bachelor's degree from an accredited school or university
- Minimum 3 years' experience as president of a company
- Minimum 5 years' experience in a service industry

SPECIAL REQUIREMENTS

- Occasional night and weekend work
- Ability to lift 30 lbs. from floor level

High-performance habit: Create focused job descriptions for every job in your business.

Implement an effective performance management system

A job description is a general description of a role in your business. It can be used for clarifying the accountability and authority of a job, as well as for recruiting employees for a job. To get maximum individual performance in your business, hire good people and then tie their success to the success of the business through a great performance management system.

This effective performance management system needs to be:

1. Simple, so people can understand it.
2. Brief, so people will use it.
3. Tied to the goals of the business, so everyone has an incentive to succeed together.

The individual performance management form that I've found to work best:

1. Employs SMART goals (see Chapter 8).
2. Is arrived at by consensus of the supervisor and the supervisee.
3. Is revisited at least every six months.

The performance management form itself includes these six items:

1. A brief statement of the future vision of the business. Example: "To be the world's leading provider of dog biscuits by June 1, 1982."
2. A brief statement of the future vision of the supervisee. Example: "To become a full equity partner by June 1, 1982."
3. A brief statement of the current three to five strategic goals of the business. Example: "Improve domestic market share to 60% by June 1, 1982."
4. Supervisor and supervisee ratings of the measurable performance goals of the individual toward achieving these strategic goals. Example: "Improve gross sales by 20% by December 31, 1981."
5. Supervisor and supervisee ratings of the individual's performance in exemplifying the core values of the business. Example: "Demonstrates integrity by doing what she says she will do."
6. Supervisor and supervisee ratings of the individual's achievement of his professional development goals toward achieving his personal future vision and the future vision of the business. Examples: Assertiveness, Sales skills, Strategic thinking and planning skills.

I favor a 5-point rating scale for supervisor and supervisee ratings:

1 = Unacceptable performance
2 = Below-average performance
3 = Average performance
4 = Above-average performance
5 = Exceptional performance

High-performance habit: Implement an individual performance management system that aligns individual goals and development with overall business goals.

High-Performance Habits Checklist

☐ Understand that you can't hold a team accountable—only individuals.

☐ Make sure all your followers know their roles and what they're accountable for.

☐ Don't hold your followers accountable for the performance of their team mates unless they have the managerial position authority to do so.

☐ Design your organizational structure to fit your business needs and goals.

☐ Create focused job descriptions for every job in your business.

☐ Implement an individual performance management system that aligns individual goals and development with overall business goals.

How can you morph from having the strength of an average person to being stronger than Hercules? It's easy, "Doc"trine #10 teaches you how to leverage your time and talent by delegating effectively.

"DOC"TRINE #10: DELEGATE

Stop trying to be God and ask for help.

The Payoff

You're getting a lot more done because you've leveraged your time and talents wisely (and now you're not up at all hours burning the midnight oil).

"Doc"trine #10 in Action: It's 10pm. Do you know where your leaders are?

It was 10pm at the large government agency, and the senior leadership staff meeting that had started at 4pm was still in session. The startling thing was that this wasn't a rare crisis that required extraordinary measures; it was a regular practice. As you can imagine, the vice presidents were denied any chance for a balanced and happy career (or life).

Two other facts stood out. First, the meeting agenda consisted primarily of the highly paid president talking non-stop while the vice presidents sat in tortured silence and listened to seemingly endless pontification about how things needed to be improved—but without the opportunity to engage in dialogue about *how* to improve things.

Second, there were no fewer than *15 vice presidents* sitting around the table; a large and unwieldy size for a senior leadership team. While at first blush these meetings may have seemed like an effort to improve accountability in the major functional areas of the agency, it proved to be a system that the president had engineered to avoid empowering his followers and to make it easier for him to micro-manage the organization.

The vice presidents had pleaded with the board for help, and many were considering leaving. The poor performance of the agency was under fire from all angles, and the media delighted in pointing out the absurdities of the situation.

The board's original directive when bringing me in was to improve the performance of the agency. After some fact finding, my initial recommendation was to replace the president because he was missing several essential skills necessary for success in his position. Not the least of these skills was the ability to release his death grip and stop over–controlling everything in the agency. In other words, he needed to delegate managerial authority. I wasn't convinced that he had the necessary perspective and potential to make the needed changes in his leadership style required to be truly successful.

The board asked me to work with the president and senior team to try to improve the situation, which we did for several months. Ultimately, the president resigned due to the constant failures and negative feedback.

While temporarily disruptive, this situation was one of the greatest achievements of my career in terms of contributing to the greater good. The president was replaced by a new leader who not only delegated and empowered his followers, but he did a fantastic job in elevating the agency to new levels of happiness, financial success, and serving the public good. And, thank goodness, no more 10pm staff meetings!

Don't be the "pinch point"

Peter Drucker (1973) famously said, "Most of what we call management consists of making it difficult for people to get their work done." Put another way, leaders need to get out of their own way. If they don't, their businesses suffer.

As their organizations grow in size and complexity, they just can't do all the jobs required any longer (not effectively). Practicing role flexibility, which was a great strength in the early days of the business, becomes a weakness in a larger and more complex business. These types of organizations work better with greater role specialization, i.e., individuals not "wearing as many hats."

Delegating is a challenge for many leaders. They often have two main fears:

1.   Fear of "losing control" of the quality of their product or service by entrusting others to do important jobs.
2.   Fear of not being valuable to the business (and therefore easily replaced) if they aren't directly producing, i.e., if they're working "on" the business instead of "in" the business.

Moving past these unrealistic fears is essential to taking any business to the next level of success. Leaders' reach truly should exceed their grasp, and always keep in mind the quote from our wise unknown guru, "For true peace of mind, resign as Master of the Universe."

Furthermore, many leaders don't possess the specialized skills necessary to run a large, complex organization, skills that are significantly different than those required to run a small business. Regardless of their business sector, I always encourage my clients to "think like an entrepreneur." Would you hire you to play the role you're playing in your business? As an entrepreneur, if you're not an "A" player in your current role, wouldn't you be better served to hire someone as soon as you can afford it? For that matter, can you really afford not to?

When you delegate effectively, everybody wins. You leverage your time and talents better, and create greater happiness and success for yourself and the person you delegate to, all leading to doing more good. Besides, how are the folks you supervise ever going to become better leaders if you don't give them a chance to lead?

In our case study for this chapter, the president's personal insecurities led him to over control every function of a huge government organization. In doing so, he was working much harder than smarter by demanding that everyone work incredibly long hours while getting extremely poor results. In addition, he was creating unnecessary turnover in the leadership ranks because good leaders won't stay in this kind of situation. Would you?

High-performance habit: Address your personal insecurities so they don't keep you from delegating effectively.

Choose your decision-making style wisely

While taking a bit of artistic license with Vroom and Yetton's (1973) work on decision making, I see four basic decision-making styles:

1.   <u>Autocratic:</u> the leader decides alone.
2.   <u>Consultative:</u> the leader consults others and then decides.
3.   <u>Consensus:</u> the team doesn't proceed until everyone agrees.
4.   <u>Democratic:</u> the team makes decision by majority vote.

So, which style do you think is the most effective way to make decisions in your business? It depends on the situation, right? For example, you certainly don't need to call a meeting of the leadership team to achieve a consensus on how many paper clips you're going to order this year.

Overall, I recommend using the consultative model of decision making most often. It provides the right balance between "people support what they help create" and "you can't hold a team accountable."

Achieving consensus is a wonderful tool in the right situations, but there are times when it's better for the whole team if the leader moves quickly and decisively. In fact, an overreliance on consensus is one of the five dysfunctions of a team (Patrick Lencioni, 2002). As a rule of thumb, do what's best for the greater good.

My experience has been that regularly using the democratic method of decision making is a formula for disaster. Just like all families, business "families" need wise leaders to survive and flourish. Often, it's not wise to give junior leaders (i.e., the "kids") an equal vote on decisions that are important for the well-being of the entire business (i.e., "family).

High-performance habit: Choose the consultative decision-making style for the majority of your leadership decisions.

Choose RAG(s) over riches

To remind myself of the major things that people really want at work, I like the "RAG(s) over riches" mnemonic. After being paid fair market value, people want:

1. Recognition for a job well done
2. Autonomy to do their jobs their way
3. Growth opportunities

Note that two out of the three come under the category of delegation— enough said. For a more detailed discussion of the things that make followers happy and motivated, refer back to "Doc"trine #1: Harness Happiness.

High-performance habit: After paying your followers fair market value, use "soft" rewards such as autonomy and growth opportunities to motivate them.

How to delegate

When I hear leaders say they're having trouble delegating, my first question is "Do you have people who you're confident you can delegate to?" It's always possible leaders are being overly fearful or controlling, but maybe they don't have employees who have a reasonable chance of doing the job well. If this is the case, then please go back to chapters 5 and 6 and re-read how to recruit and retain good people and then put them in roles that play to their strengths. Problem solved. (To improve your delegation skills, keep the checklist at the end of this chapter handy.)

High-performance habit: Delegate clear goals and enough authority to succeed to competent people.

High-Performance Habits Checklist

- ☐ Address your personal insecurities so they don't keep you from delegating effectively.
- ☐ Choose the consultative decision-making style for the majority of your leadership decisions.
- ☐ After paying your followers fair market value, use "soft" rewards such as autonomy and growth opportunities to motivate them.
- ☐ Delegate clear goals and enough authority to succeed to competent people.
- ☐ Only delegate to people you feel confident can do the job. If you don't have those people, then hire some.
- ☐ Delegate clear responsibility and accountability with measurable goals.
- ☐ Delegate enough authority to get the job done. Accountability without authority is a sure setup for failure.

Now that we've got the foundation in place, in "Doc"trine #11 we explore how you can build that impressive mansion on the hill called "teamwork.."

"DOC"TRINE #11: CREATE TEAMWORK

Even Michael Jordan couldn't win without a strong team around him.

The Payoff

Your business thrives because you know strong teamwork produces a great deal more than just the sum of individual team members' efforts (and now you know just about anything is possible for your future).

"Doc"trine #11 in Action: In Teams We Trust

A professional services firm was struggling to attract and retain good business developers. These employees were expected to bring in new clients and then keep those clients happy, and the firm had a difficult time finding advisors who did both really well. This led to a high level of unhealthy turnover (as opposed to healthy turnover, in which the people who aren't going to be successful anyway leave).

After a thorough assessment, we realized we didn't have enough strong sales people to make this model, the individual-producer-"eat-what-you- kill" model, work successfully. We decided to change the firm's service model by creating teams comprised of specialized "Finders," "Minders," and "Grinders." Each team was led by a strong business developer, a Finder; included a strong customer service representative, a Minder; and also included some dedicated administrative staff, Grinders.

The results were impressive. Sales, customer service, employee morale, and employee retention all increased dramatically. The firm's leadership team realized it was very difficult to find individuals who could play multiple roles well, but that it was relatively easy to assemble a team of people who together could do everything exceptionally well.

Create synergy in your team

It's well documented that a high-performing team can accomplish more than the sum of its members' individual efforts. It's called synergy, and it's easily illustrated by the equation $1 + 1 + 1 = 5$. A team that works together effectively can achieve more as a group than the sum of its individual members' achievements.

Sports examples abound. I particularly admire Phil Jackson, who is widely acknowledged as the best professional basketball coach ever. He was a master at molding a group of individually talented players with strong egos (e.g., Michael Jordan, Kobe Bryant, and Dennis Rodman) into high-performing championship teams. He was able to convince his hyper-competitive star players that becoming part of a high-performing team would enable them to win championships—something they had been unable to do before.

I don't care how good you are and how hard you work, you just can't beat another whole team by yourself, in sports or in business. If you aren't a good team player now, you better learn how to be one if you want to win at the game of business.

High-performance habit: Use teamwork to overcome the limitations of individual achievement.

Do you have a leadership team or a leadership committee?

To extend the basketball analogy, have you ever seen a basketball team play a game in which the center won the game but the guard lost? The idea seems silly, doesn't it? Well, isn't that similar to a leadership team in which the Vice President of Sales has a good year and the Vice President of Human Resources has a bad one? Since they're both members of the same team, in the grand scheme of things shouldn't they be winning or losing together? If they're not, then you have a leadership committee, not a leadership team. Make your team a true team whose win-lose outcomes are tied together.

In our case-study firm, individual employees' compensation plans had both an individual component and a team component. In this way we wanted to encourage individual achievement within an overall framework of team achievement (more on this concept later).

High-performance habit: Make sure you have a leadership team rather than a leadership committee by creating a culture in which your followers win and lose together.

Schedule recurring teamwork events

Don't leave communication and teamwork to chance; structure it into your business' schedule. Here are some suggestions:

1. **Daily**: A fifteen minute huddle in each work team focused on tactical priorities for the day.
2. **Weekly**: A staff meeting focused on tactical priorities for the week.
3. **Monthly**: A strategic dashboard update meeting focused on strategic priorities and priority actions.
4. **Quarterly**: A deeper-dive strategic update meeting including future trend updates, a SWOT Analysis, and a Leading Indicator Evaluation ™.
5. **Yearly**: A full scale strategic review to revisit all current assumptions and data.

High-performance habit: Schedule regular events to fully leverage the advantages of teamwork in your business.

Promote teamwork with your compensation plan

Be careful about what you reward, because that's exactly what you'll get. For example, if you create an eat-what-you-kill culture (like the one in our case study) that rewards individual achievement, you'll get high levels of individual achievement. However, you'll also get hoarding behaviors (to guard against someone else "stealing" a client, for example) and you'll see little interest in helping others through teamwork. (Why would you? It's merely a distraction from what is rewarded.) Therefore, under this compensation structure it's almost impossible to enjoy the payoffs of a high level of teamwork.

While specific compensation programs are beyond the scope of this book, I recommend that you pay your followers for two basic components of their performance:

1. Individual performance: not for longevity, and not because the individual is a member of your biological family, but actual achievement.
2. Team performance: contribution to the overall success of the business.

This approach rewards individuals for their individual results, as well as incentivizing them to be good team players so the whole business does well.

High-performance habit: Reward both individual achievement and teamwork in your compensation plan.

For maximum motivation, use "open book" management

Sharing any aspect of their financials seems to scare the living daylights out of many leaders. Mostly it seems they're concerned about their followers disapproving of how much money they (the leaders) make. This surprises me. What are the followers going to do, fire the leader? I think this situation provides an opportunity for the leaders to inspire their followers on how they, too, can make more money by making a greater contribution to the business. This and a considerable number of other upsides exist that justify sharing your basic financials, aka "open book management" (Case, 1995).

As mentioned earlier, I've heard more than a few leaders complain that their employees are lazy and don't care about the business. But if we talk a little longer I usually discover that these leaders pay their employees as little as possible, give them very little autonomy in doing their jobs, and share little or no information about how the company is doing financially. I'm sure that under these circumstances I'd be biting at the bit to do my very best for this business. Wouldn't you? I hope you're a fan of sarcasm...

But seriously, my thinking is clear: If you want your employees to care, then you need to give them a reason to care. For one thing, you can practice open book management. That is, you can share enough about the financials of the business that your employees see how their efforts affect the success of the whole organization. Then they can get excited about moving the financial success needle, just as you are. Once again, what terrible thing is going to happen if your employees know about the basic finances of your business?

High-performance habit: Employ open book management to maximize engagement and motivation among your followers.

High-Performance Habits Checklist

☐ Use teamwork to overcome the limitations of individual achievement.

☐ Make sure you have a leadership team rather than a leadership committee by creating a culture in which your followers win and lose together.

☐ Schedule regular events to leverage the advantages of teamwork fully in your business.

☐ Reward both individual achievement and teamwork in your compensation plan.

☐ Employ open book management to maximize engagement and motivation among your followers.

Now you've got a great system for achieving business results, but how are you going to adapt to the changing business conditions in the world around you? "Doc"trine #12 shows you how to build continuous innovation into your business culture.

"DOC"TRINE #12: INSTITUTIONALIZE INNOVATION

You can't outrun change—it's faster than you.

The Payoff

Your business changes, adapts, and continues to be successful. And you realize you've created a one-of-a-kind perpetual-motion happiness, money, and doing good machine.

"Doc"trine #12 in Action: The Game Changers

The leadership team of a major manufacturing company wanted to grow the company aggressively, and they were debating whether to focus their expansion efforts within North America or internationally. After much discussion, they decided to focus domestically. They adopted a new strategy to help them win the upcoming competition to become the primary supplier to a major domestic retailer. Winning the competition would result in a huge leap in sales volume.

At past competitions, each manufacturer sent two or three representatives to a multi-day conference. At this conference, the competing teams submitted bids for the business based on the specifications of the retailer. Our leadership team began to brainstorm ways that they could change the game and win the competition.

They sent 12 people to the conference. They carefully included experts on every conceivable aspect of the bidding process, and they were extremely aggressive in their bids. One night the team worked all night to come back to the table the next morning with a bid that was still profitable but qualitatively and quantitatively superior to the bids of their competitors. They won the competition hands down, and overnight they became the largest domestic supplier of their product. They won the game by changing the way it was played—through innovation.

Build innovation into your business culture

You only have to look around you to see the need for continuous innovation in your business. Will Rogers said it best, "Even if you're on the right track, you'll get run over if you just sit there." Look at Eastman Kodak—it didn't innovate fast enough from film photography to digital photography. Sony, Panasonic, and Sharp, some of the Japanese behemoths in home electronics hardware, are falling behind to Samsung and others that are more in touch with the needs of today's consumers. Computer manufacturers like Dell and Hewlett Packard are struggling as more people move to tablets and smart phones to access the web. Print publications such as city newspapers are folding at a rapid rate because people have begun to prefer their news in digital form. Buggy whips, anyone?

Businesses go through a natural cycle of growth, leveling off, and decline as their market matures and competition increases (see figure below).

JUMPING THE S-CURVE

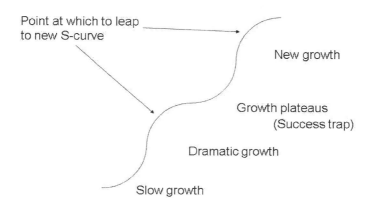

Through a structured program of innovation, businesses can "jump" over the phases of slowing and decline to the next phase of growth. This is called "jumping the 'S' curve" (Nunez & Breene, 2011), and it may require reinventing the business as consumer needs change and evolve. Without a structured program of continuous innovation, the business likely will experience inconsistent growth at best or bankruptcy at worst. Remember how the leadership team in our case study decided to accelerate the growth of the business by changing their normal growth process?

High-performance habit: Constantly adapt your business to keep pace with a constantly changing world around you.

Problem solving and innovation are quite different processes (Robert & Weiss, 1988). As you can see from the figure below, problem solving involves restoring performance to its previous level. Innovation means taking performance to a higher level, and it often requires initiative from a leader. The key point here is that innovation is not a passive process. Sometimes it's difficult and even scary, and innovation usually requires

conscious effort from the leader. The leaders in our case study made a conscious decision to do things very differently in order to take the performance of the business to a whole new level.

PROBLEM SOLVING VS. INNOVATION

High-performance habit: As a leader it is your responsibility to create a culture of innovation in your team.

Despite what you may read in the business press, organizations don't change—people do (Haines, 2007). Keep this in mind as you strive for innovation in your business and create a change management system that focuses on helping individuals to change. Any change in your business will be the net result of many individuals changing within it.

People support what they help create—empower them to be creative

Get the right followers involved on the front end of any change effort. These people are usually the ones who best understand the work involved and have valuable expertise. People take pride in their own efforts, and even though the original planning is likely to take longer, the implementation and success of the change effort will be a slam dunk.

If you want your employees to be creative, they must have your permission to fail. Yes, you heard that correctly. If they don't have permission to fail, then they don't really have permission to innovate to succeed either. In other words, if you want to build a culture of continuous innovation in your business, people need to feel comfortable trying new things, and in order to feel comfortable trying new things, they need to know that if their idea fails, they won't be punished.

Some organizations give a "Turkey of the Year" award to the idea that fails the biggest (a great project for your Chief Fun Officer). This sends a clear message that you value innovation and reasoned risk taking, and that you don't expect every idea to be a home run. This will not only increase innovation but also happiness within your organization, which will increase profits and doing good. See how this all works together?

Of course you don't want your employees to make the same mistakes repeatedly, but if you want innovation, your employees must be allowed to take risks and make mistakes. Peter Drucker said, "The better a man is, the more mistakes will he make - for the more new things he will try. I would never promote a man into a top level job who had not made mistakes, and big ones at that. Otherwise, he is sure to be mediocre." (Please excuse Mr. Drucker's sexist language; it was a different time).

High-performance habit: People support what they help create, so empower your followers to be creative and to fail sometimes.

Take moderate business risks most of the time

Sure, there are times when it makes sense to swing for the fence, but plenty of research shows that those who are consistently successful over time tend to take moderate risks (see figure below).

OPTIMUM RISK TAKING FOR SUSTAINED SUCCESS

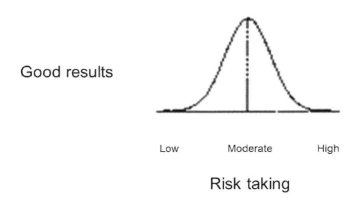

Good results

Low   Moderate   High

Risk taking

In my work, I've seen time and again that there are always more good ideas than resources to pursue them. How then do you decide which initiatives to pursue? Consider these criteria when evaluating implementing a potential innovation:

1.   Is it a good fit with our overall strategy?
2.   What is the potential positive impact?
3.   What is the cost in time and money?
4.   How much risk are we taking?

You can assess these factors in a number of ways. For example, in this era of "big data," you can generate sophisticated algorithms and computer models. If you don't have the resources for this kind of effort, use a 0-10 scale where, for example, 0 is "no risk," 5 is "moderate risk," and 10 is "very high risk" to evaluate potential innovations.

For an innovation you are considering, generate a 0-10 rating on each of the four factors above, and then examine the totaled score. If you want to get more detailed, you can assign weights to each factor: e.g., "we will weight risk as 30% of the prediction equation and cost in time and money as 10%. This basic method of thinking through your options is infinitely better than proceeding without any significant analytical thinking and discussion.

For example, in a strategic planning meeting with a small start-up business, we were considering hiring a well-paid salesperson to the team. We had an opportunity to capture significant additional new revenue, but there was also financial risk because it would take several months for that new revenue to come in. The ratings for the potential change looked like this:

1. Fit with strategy = 9
2. Potential positive impact = 8
3. Costs = $150,000 salary, individual assessment by Terry Dockery (candidate already identified), travel costs for local interviews, time required for local interviews and discussions
4. Risk = 7, due to cash flow impact for three to four months

We decided this change was a relatively high risk, but all the positives involved made it a risk worth taking. The salesperson was on the road closing deals a few short weeks later.

High-performance habit: For sustained success, take moderate business risks most of the time.

Build some "slack" into your business

Too many businesses buy the myth of "working at 110%." First, to state the obvious, it's physically impossible to do anything more than 100%. This kind of rah-rah hype just sets people and businesses up for failure. Leave this destructive, manic drivel behind and work at about 85% of full capacity. That way you leave time and energy for:

1. Innovating
2. Solving the inevitable, unanticipated problems that arise
3. Taking advantage of inevitable, unanticipated opportunities that arise

This is an instance of being more proactive than reactive, and working smarter—not harder. The leadership team from our case study had the capacity and flexibility to take 12 people out of their day-to-day duties and attend a multi-day event, and it paid off handsomely for them.

High-performance habit: Build some "slack" into your business so you can easily adapt to fluctuations and take advantage of opportunities.

How to be creative through brainstorming

Brainstorming, if done well, is a great group exercise to generate ideas for potential innovations. Remember, all innovations start off as ideas in someone's head that are later fine-tuned. If done poorly, however, brainstorming actually can hurt creativity and innovation. The end goal is to get your fun-loving and creative juices flowing and to generate and capture as many ideas as possible. You can evaluate them later, but you'll limit your creativity and good ideas if you combine evaluation with idea generation. So don't. Follow these guidelines for effective brainstorming:

1. Be creative & suspend judgment
2. There is NO idea too outrageous
3. Quantity now leads to quality later
4. "Yes and" instead of "yes but"
5. Piggyback on others' ideas

Once you've brainstormed all the ideas you can, evaluate them to decide which ideas to commit your time and resources to. In our case study, what if when the original idea was presented someone had said, "I think taking 12 people to the competition is a stupid idea. What else have you got?"

Some research suggests that brainstorming can be even more effective if people have a chance to generate ideas on their own before coming together in a group session. Use this tool as well when the situation allows it.

High-performance habit: To inspire creativity through brainstorming, separate idea generation and evaluation.

Schedule recurring innovation events

Because its message is so powerful, I want to revisit a section from Chapter 11 on teamwork. Remember those scheduled events to build teamwork into your business culture? Why not use those same events to include an innovation component? It can be as simple as asking, "What can we improve?" or as complex as our case-study team's approach to changing the way the game is played.

1. **Daily**: A 15-minute "huddle" in each work team focused on tactical priorities for the day.
2. **Weekly**: A staff meeting addressing tactical priorities for the week.
3. **Monthly**: A strategic dashboard update meeting on strategic priorities and priority actions.
4. **Quarterly**: A deeper-dive strategic update meeting including future trend updates, a SWOT Analysis, and a Leading Indicator Evaluation ™.
5. **Yearly**: A full-scale strategic review that revisits all current assumptions and data.

High-performance habit: Make recurring innovation events a part of your business culture.

Plan for things to get harder before they get easier

Even the most positive change can be trying at times, especially in the middle portion. In fact, you can think of it as the death of the old way followed by the birth of the new. No doubt you already know that these are emotionally intense activities. Set your expectations accordingly, and resist any temptation to put on your rose-colored glasses.

Elizabeth Kubler-Ross (1969) listed the five stages of dramatic change and emotional upheaval in her book, On Death and Dying. The five stages are:

1. **Denial**: "This stressful event isn't really happening."
2. **Anger**: "I don't like that I have to go through this stressful event."
3. **Bargaining**: "What do I need to do to get out of this stressful event?"
4. **Depression**: "Things are always going to be this stressful."
5. **Acceptance**: "This isn't so bad; it may be okay."

Stephen Haines (2007) called this the "rollercoaster of change." Basically, during change things tend to get more difficult before they get easier.

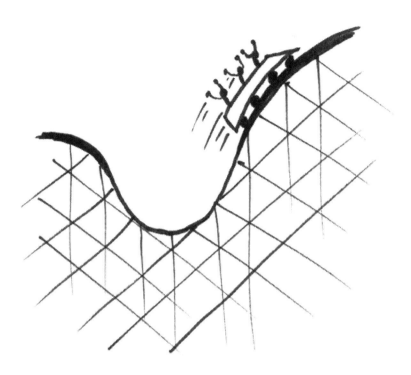

Here are three tips for managing change:

1. **Communicate**: Early on, address people's fears, get their input, and set realistic expectations.
2. **Communicate**: In the middle, share concerns, especially after the initial excitement wears off and people enter the doldrums of fatigue and more fear.
3. **Communicate**: At the end, celebrate and give credit. People should start to believe that they thought it was a good idea all along.

High-performance habit: Persevere when making changes for performance improvement—things are usually more difficult before they get easier.

High-Performance Habits Checklist

- ☐ Constantly adapt your business to keep pace with a constantly changing world around you.
- ☐ As a leader, your responsibility is to create a culture of innovation in your team.
- ☐ People support what they help create, so empower your followers to be creative and to fail sometimes.
- ☐ For sustained success, take moderate business risks most of the time.
- ☐ Build some "slack" into your business so you can easily adapt to fluctuations and take advantage of opportunities.
- ☐ To inspire creativity through brainstorming, separate idea generation and evaluation.
- ☐ Make recurring innovation events a part of your business culture.
- ☐ Persevere when making changes for performance improvement—things are usually more difficult before they get easier.

EPILOGUE

I hope that you've enjoyed this book and trust that it's given you the tools you need to be happier, make more money, and do more good out there in the business world. Circling back to the opening pages, I'll repeat the promise that started your journey through these ideas: I promise that if you implement the 12 "Doc"trines, you'll achieve these things, and likely get some additional benefits that you can't even imagine right now. Business karma is still alive and well and touching lives every day.

I'll leave you with one of my favorite stories. A family business had experienced flat sales for a period of time. Much worse than that, however, was the relationship between the father and son. When I arrived on the scene, they had become so estranged they literally hadn't spoken in many months.

I could tell you how we made personnel and structural changes, and how we conducted teambuilding, training, and planning meetings to increase revenue significantly. Yes, we did all those things and everyone was happier, made more money, and felt good about what the business provided in the world. But that's not the best outcome we achieved.

At the end of one especially productive conflict resolution meeting between the father and son, two things happened that hadn't occurred in at least 20 years. The dad hugged his son and told him he loved him. Now, was the process worth it? Did it make these two men happier and bring them closer? Definitely, but furthermore they show that being happier, making more money, and doing more good is right in front of you—all you need to do is reach out and embrace them.

The 12 "Doc"trines:

1. Harness happiness
2. Be someone worth following
3. Focus your vision
4. Value your values
5. Field a pro team
6. Don't Turn Eagles Into Turkeys
7. Win with win-win
8. Measure success

9.   Clarify roles and accountability
10. Delegate
11. Create teamwork
12. Institutionalize innovation

If I can be helpful, please don't hesitate to get in touch. Go forth and be happy, make money, and do good!

Terry "Doc" Dockery, Ph.D.
www.businesspsychology.com

REFERENCES

Berne, E. (1964*). Games People Play – The Basic Hand Book of Transactional Analysis*. New York, NY: Ballantine Books.

Case, J. (1995). *Open-book management: The coming business revolution*. New York, NY: HarperCollins.

Covey, S. (1992). *The Seven Habits of Highly Effective People*. New York, NY: Simon & Schuster.

Covey, S., Merrill, A. & Merrill, R. (1994) *First Things First: To Live, to Love, to Learn, to Leave a Legacy*. New York, NY: Simon and Schuster.

Doran, G. T. (1981). There's a S.M.A.R.T. way to write management's goals and objectives. *Management Review, Volume 70* (11), 35–36.

Drucker, P. (1973) *Management Tasks, Responsibilities and Practices*. New York, NY: Harper & Row.

Drucker, P. (2001). *The Essential Drucker*. New York, NY: Harper Business.

McGregor, D. (1960). *The Human Side of Enterprise*. New York, NY: McGraw-Hill.

Freud, S. (1910). *The origin and development of psychoanalysis, American Journal of Psychology 21(2)*, 196–218.

Haines, S. 2000. *The Complete Guide to Systems Thinking and Learning*. San Diego, CA: Haines Centre Press.

Haines, S. (2007). *ABC's of Strategic Management*, San Diego, CA: Haines Centre Press.

Haines, S. (2007). *Strategic Planning Simplified: The Systems Thinking Approach to Building High Performance Teams and Organizations*. San Diego, CA: Systems Thinking Press.

Humphrey, A. (2005). SWOT analysis for management consulting. *SRI Alumni Newsletter*, SRI International.

Janis, I. L. (1972). *Victims of Groupthink: a Psychological Study of Foreign-Policy Decisions and Fiascoes*. Boston, MA: Houghton Mifflin.

Karpman, S. (1968). Fairy tales and script analysis. *Transactional Analysis Bulletin*, 7(26), 39-43.

Kübler-Ross E. (1969). *On Death and Dying*. London: Macmillan.

Lencioni, P. (2002). *The Five Dysfunctions of a Team*, San Francisco, CA: Jossey-Bass.

Maslow, A. H. (1943). A theory of human motivation. *Psychological Review*, 50(4), 370–396.

Mauborgne, R. & Kim, W. (2005). *Blue Ocean Strategy*. Boston, MA: Harvard Business Press.

McChesney, C., Covey S. & Huling, J. (2012). *The 4 Disciplines of Execution: Achieving Your Wildly Important Goals*. New York, NY: Free Press.

Newton, D. A. (1994). *Feed Your Eagles*. Irwin Professional Publishing.

Nunez, P. & Breene, T. (2011). *Jumping the S Curve: How to Beat the Growth Cycle, Get on Top, and Stay There*. Boston, MA: Harvard Business Review Press.

Ohio State Leadership Studies (1945-1970's).

Robert, M. & Weiss, A. (1988). *The Innovation Formula*. New York, NY: Harper & Row.

Seligman, M. E. P. (1975). Helplessness: *On Depression, Development, and Death*. San Francisco, CA: W. H. Freeman.

Thomas, K. W., & Kilmann, R. H. (1974). *Thomas-Kilmann Conflict Mode Instrument*. Mountain View, CA: Xicom, a subsidiary of CPP, Inc.

Tuckman, B. (1965). Developmental sequence in small groups. *Psychological Bulletin*, 63 (6): 384–399.

Vroom, V. H, & Yetton, P. W. (1973). *Leadership and Decision-Making*. Pittsburgh, PA: University of Pittsburgh Press.

INDEX

A

"A" Players 71; identifying 77-78; PIES 79; how to hire 81-83
Accountability 124-126
Achievers, 3 levels 78-80
All Stars 71

B

Balance 23-24
BARB technique 102-103
Behavior, 2 ways to change 99-102
Blind spots 46-48
Blue Ocean strategy 61-62
Brainstorming 152-153

C

"Car" exercise 59
Career choices 25-26
Change 154; rollercoaster of 155
Cheerleaders 71
Chief Fun Officer 34-35
Coaching, how to 82-84
Compensation 141-143
Conflict, right amount 93-94; "I" in team 94, Decision Tree 96; Management Styles 96-99
Core success measures 116-117
Core values, foundation 67; how to create 70; driving results 70-71
Customers, happy 38

D

Dashboard, strategic 117-118
Dead wood 71
Decision making styles 136
Delegation 134-135, how to 138

Differentiation 63-64
Drama Triangle 36-38

E

Eagles, feed 76-77
Emotional bank account 30-31
Energy vampires 80-81

F

Financial Performance Prediction Model 109-111
Focus, on the positive, 21-22; on what you can control 22-23; on what is important 55-57

G

Glacial progress 51
Goal setting, achievable 57-58
Greed 68-70
Group development stages 91-92

H

Happiness, harnessing 17-19
Happiness, 5 things that create 24-25, 34
Human motivation, secret to 27-30

I

Innovation, culture of 146; versus problem-solving 147-148; people support what they create 148-150, recurring events 153-154

J

Jack Welch Grid 71-72
Job descriptions 128-130
Johari Window 46-47
Jumping the S curve 146-147

K

Kiss Principle, revised 54-55

L

Lead by example 44
Leading Indicator Evaluation 115-116
Leader Trickle Down Law 42-43
Leaders as parents 41-42
Leadership success, 2 best predictors 31-32
Leadership team vs. committee 140-141

M

Measurement, cycle 108
Mission statement 62-63

N

Need Hierarchy 32-33
New skills, acquiring 84

O

Open book management 142-143
Organizational Energy System 51-52
Organizational structure 126-128

P

Perfectionism, overcoming 57-58
Performance management 130-131
PIES 78
Primary pleasures 32
Principle of Balance & Justification 23-24
Pro team, benefits 76-77
Profit-Stealers 49-50

R

RAGS over riches 137
Religion-based business 72-73
Retirement myth 27
Risk taking 150
Role fit, importance 86-87; firing to help succeed 88-89

S

Sales techniques 104
Self-confidence, increasing 38
Self-fulfilling prophecy 20-22
SKEPTIC model 111-113
Skills, acquiring new 85
"Slack" in your business 151-152
SMART goals 64-65
Standard setting 58-59
Strategic priorities 64
Strategic priority actions 64-65; 118-119; 150-151
Strategy and tactics, balanced 53
Stress and performance 35-36
SWOT analysis 113-114
Synergy 139-140

T

Teamwork events, recurring 141
"Terrorists" 71
Theory X& Y 34-35

Three-sixty degree feedback 120-122

Time management 55-57

Trust-profit connection 45-46

Truth, power of 43-44

U

Urgent vs. important 55-57

V

Values/results grid 71-72

Vision, brainstorming technique 59-60

Vision statement 60

W

WIFM 94

ABOUT THE AUTHOR

Terry "Doc" Dockery, Ph.D. (yes, Dr. "Doc" Dockery) is a licensed business psychologist, writer, and speaker who has helped leaders be happier and more successful since 1993. He specializes in creating dramatic revenue growth without undue stress or risk.

Dr. Dockery lives in Atlanta, Georgia, and his proudest accomplishment is his happy family. In his spare time he sings and plays harmonica in a blues and rock band. His band won the Lucille Award from BB King in 1988.

31754962R00094

Made in the USA
Charleston, SC
28 July 2014